colonial

Switzerland's
Global
Entanglements

Swiss National Museum

Scheidegger & Spiess

Introductions

Essays

Emblem of imperial power

The pith helmet is an emblem of colonial rule. It was worn by *white* men and women—always together with white clothing—to protect against the sun and other dangers. However, the colonial dress code also served to set them apart from the local population.

Pith helmet, probably Congo, late nineteenth century, Musée d'ethnographie de Genève (MEG), photo: M. Johnathan Watts.

Preface

Denise Tonella

Director, Swiss National Museum

After mostly ignoring the topic for a long time, coming to terms with the colonial past has increasingly found its way into public consciousness, not least in Switzerland. Not only have researchers in various fields published work on the issue, it is also the subject of intense discussion in society. The scope of the debates is wide and opinions diverge on multiple details. Because Switzerland perceives itself as a neutral state, colonialism remains a challenging topic for the country's collective memory.

At the Swiss National Museum, the exhibition *colonial—Switzerland's Global Entanglements* addresses a wide audience and intends to offer a framework for understanding and evaluating the current discussions. Switzerland's colonial entanglements were numerous, and the colonial system and its way of thinking has left its mark on the population as a whole. The Swiss National Museum sees its role as informing the public about this aspect of Swiss history and its transnational dimension, and inspiring people to gain a deeper understanding of the subject. We want our visitors to join in the discussion on a sensitive topic that also touches on unhealed social wounds. To that end, we reassess and identify links between historical sources, highlighting aspects of contemporary relevance, and provide space for artistic interpretations and perspectives from different continents. The exhibition is dedicated to providing a nuanced discussion of Swiss history in which many different voices can be heard. The period being addressed begins in the late fifteenth century and ends with topical questions about the colonial dimensions of remembrance, language, and consumption in Switzerland.

This publication accompanies the exhibition, providing an introduction to the traces of colonial heritage in the holdings of the Swiss National Museum while also discussing fundamental ideas and links with colonial history and the ways in which Switzerland was, and still is, entangled. The ten essays below take the reader through the exhibition's main focus areas. Taking as their starting point traces of colonialism in everyday life in Switzerland, they examine the trade in enslaved people; the phenomenon of mercenary soldiers; the (transit) trade in goods; the exploitation of nature and the environment; racism; missionary societies; and Swiss scholarly researchers in colonial settings. The essay section concludes with discussions of the structural consequences of colonialism in the Global South; the role of museums as colonial archives; and Swiss diplomatic relations during the phase of decolonisation. It is followed by a richly illustrated section showcasing some of the exhibits on display.

Neither the exhibition nor the present publication would have been possible without the efforts of the curators Marina Amstad, Pascale Meyer, Raphael Schwere, and Marilyn Umurungi, to whom I should like to extend my warmest thanks. Engaging with Switzerland's multifarious colonial entanglements was a challenging task, to which they applied their specialist expertise with great dedication. My sincere gratitude also goes to scenographer Alex Harb for his highly empathic and sensitive approach to the exhibition design. I should also like to thank Sophie Dänzer for her meticulous coordination of the project, and Lomotion for the discursive video installation on current debates. Special thanks are also due to the members of the international scientific advisory board for their painstaking input in formulating our concept and for sharing their indispensable expertise. I am grateful to the publisher, Scheidegger & Spiess, and to the authors of the papers collected in this volume. Finally, I want to offer my heartfelt thanks to the many institutions who generously loaned key exhibits as well as to the many other contributors, who helped to make this project a success.

Because the exhibition and book alone cannot do full justice to the topic, we have initiated a number of additional projects, on the one hand, to supplement our permanent exhibitions with information about Switzerland's colonial past, on the other, to allow us to engage with our collections more intensely, reassess objects regarding their colonial contexts, and critically examine discriminatory and racist terminology in our database. Not least, because object inventories, categorisations, and taggings also attest to the perception of the "unfamiliar", the "other", and the "exotic" and reflect colonial ideologies and power structures. The exhibition *colonial—Switzerland's Global Entanglements* thus represents a major step in a long-term process of engaging with the topic and re-examining the cultural heritage that is an intrinsic aspect of the Swiss National Museum's collection.

Exhibiting
Swiss colonial history

Marina Amstad
Pascale Meyer
Raphael Schwere
Marilyn Umurungi

Many chapters in the history of Swiss colonialism have been researched in recent years. But how can these fragments be combined to form a whole, and how can we gain an overview? Answering these questions is the stated aim of the exhibition.

Swiss colonial history extends from the sixteenth century through to the present day. While it is indeed Swiss history, rather than taking place solely on Swiss soil, it is set on all continents in a world of global networks. These are the stories of how individuals, companies, and communities in all parts of Switzerland have benefited from European colonialism. We have structured the exhibition according to the various spheres of colonial activity.

For example, there were the Swiss trading companies that were commercially involved with enslaved people in the eighteenth century. There were the mercenaries from Switzerland in the armies of colonial powers who subjugated the local population. Swiss colonial settlements, missionary work, colonial administration, and science are also sectors in which Swiss men and women played a part.

In addition to depicting the structural conditions and systematic economic exploitation of the time, the exhibition also presents people and their everyday lives, showing that there was scope for individual action, and that the colonised put up resistance. In addition, we tell of Swiss men and women who dedicated themselves to fighting for the abolition of slavery or who, as missionaries, not only preached the gospel, but also actively campaigned for education and medical care. Despite the plethora of topics, it is vital that we do proper justice to the nuances.

Racist thinking and beliefs have left their mark on Switzerland. There were the scientific instruments developed in Zurich which were used in the nineteenth century to measure the skulls of "primitive peoples" in order to prove their supposed inferiority. These, alongside the advertising posters for ethnological expositions known as "human zoos" that were still being staged as late as 1964, bear witness to notions of "exoticism" and a racist subtext about the ostensible superiority of *white* Europeans. The exhibition makes a brief foray into these case studies highlighting the history of racism in Switzerland. There is a second focal point on colonial photography and its inherent "colonial gaze" as one strand in legitimising colonial action.

Swiss men and women participated in the exploitation of nature in colonial territories. There was the father and daughter team of Bernard and Vivienne de Watteville, who hunted big game together and supplied the Natural History Museum in Bern with numerous animal skins and bones. A further piece of evidence is provided of Swiss participation in the plantation economy on Sumatra in the Dutch East Indies (now Indonesia), which is still practised in its environmentally damaging form today. Colonial continuities of this kind are also examined in the exhibition.

Marina Amstad
Pascale Meyer
Raphael Schwere
Marilyn Umurungi

Ultimately, there is an urgent need to explore colonialism precisely because colonial structures are potent enough to retain their efficacy in the twenty-first century. Decades after the formal process of decolonisation, the consequences continue to influence the lives of millions of people in the former colonies. On the blue "And today?" walls, the exhibition discusses how colonial mechanisms are manifested in our own time. We also use these surfaces to highlight processes of coming to terms with colonial trauma and injustice as a vital component of healing and reparation. There are critical flashbacks to Swiss colonial history in Sri Lanka and Indonesia, including different artistic perspectives on colonial Swiss naturalists, and in the civic sphere we hear about the people of Flores recalling a colonial massacre. This multiplicity of viewpoints must be fostered more intensively. We can only attain a complete view of this chapter of shared global history by including external voices.

Current debates are addressed in the final part of the exhibition. The diversity of opinions in these controversies acts like a kind of seismograph, reflecting the social relevance and acceptance of postcolonial issues. Should we rename streets and buildings whose names incorporate the term M—, an indicator of African ancestry today deemed offensive in German, and should the monuments to "great men" who were involved in colonialism be toppled? Visitors to the exhibition are encouraged to discuss these issues.

Bearing in mind that curatorial work invariably involves acts of omission, our choice of thematic focus is an attempt to provide an overview. Before—and while—creating this exhibition we followed the wide range of lively debate on the subject, encompassing the role of museums in colonialism as well as ways of communicating colonial history in museums today. In this context, for example, we gave extensive consideration to the degree to which problematic objects can be exhibited at all: how can we narrate colonial history through objects without perpetuating the racist and colonial attitudes attached to them? Which objects are problematic, and for whom? To address these questions, we entered into a dialogue with museums, academics, and the public in advance.

Moreover, we were able to draw on the expertise of a scientific advisory board and benefit from the knowledge of researchers, curators, and archivists in numerous bilateral discussions. We also invited civic engagement groups in Zurich and Lausanne to participate in a public critical appraisal of the exhibition concept.

Two fellows from TheMuseumsLab 2023 and students from universities in Basel, Bern, and Zurich provided helpful museological criticism. The cooperation with Institut Fondamental d'Afrique Noire (IFAN) at Cheikh Anta Diop University in Dakar made it possible to produce crucial expert videos. Thanks to the response to our call for colonial family histories, objects, and photos, we have a number of exhibits that have never before been shown in public. We are particularly grateful to all the people and institutions who participated. Furthermore, we are indebted to all the artists who entrusted us with their works for inclusion in this exhibition of cultural history as important commentaries.

At the end of the curating process—and at the end of the exhibition itself—we cannot but acknowledge that the picture of Switzerland's colonial involvement and its continuities is still incomplete. We therefore view our exhibition as a source of inspiration that lays the foundations and raises questions for in-depth discussions between the museum, its visitors, and the general public.

We have decided not to interfere with historical objects, even if they contain racist terms that are no longer used today. In descriptions and quotations, we use a dash for exonyms such as "Negro", "Moors", "Indians"—here spelt out for once for the sake of clarification—in order to avoid reproducing racist language.

David, Thomas, Bouda Etemad and Janick Marina Schaufelbuehl: *Schwarze Geschäfte: Die Beteiligung von Schweizern an Sklaverei und Sklavenhandel im 18. und 19. Jahrhundert*, Zurich: Limmat, 2005.

Debrunner, Hans Werner: *Schweizer im kolonialen Afrika*, Basel: Basler Afrika Bibliographien, 1991.

Étienne, Noémie et al. (eds.): *Exotic Switzerland? Looking Outward in the Age of Enlightenment* (exhibition catalogue Palais de Rumine, Lausanne), Zurich/Berlin: diaphanes, 2020.

Holenstein, André: *Mitten in Europa: Verflechtung und Abgrenzung in der Schweizer Geschichte*, Baden: Hier und Jetzt, 2014.

Kägi, Kaspar, and Konrad J. Kuhn: "Kolonialexpansion, fremde Dienste und Sklaverei: Jakob Christoph Zieglers (1791–1825) Briefe aus Sumatra", in *Zürcher Taschenbuch auf das Jahr 2010*, 130, 2009, pp. 71–141.

Krauer, Philipp: *Swiss Mercenaries in the Dutch East Indies: A Transimperial History of Military Labour, 1848-1914*, Leiden: Leiden University Press, 2024.

Kreis, Georg: *Blicke auf die koloniale Schweiz. Ein Forschungsbericht*, Zurich: Chronos, 2023.

Kreis, Georg: "Anders als die klassischen Kolonialmächte? Zum informellen Kolonialismus der Schweiz" in Zürcher Kunstgesellschaft/Kunsthaus Zürich (eds.): *Die Postkoloniale Schweiz*, (exhibition catalogue, Kunsthaus Zürich), Zurich, 2020, pp. 25–30.

Minder, Patrick: *La Suisse coloniale? Les représentations de l'Afrique et des Africains en Suisse au temps de colonies (1880–1939)*, Bern: Lang, 2006.

Osterhammel, Jürgen, and Jan C. Jansen: *Kolonialismus, Geschichte, Formen, Folgen*, Munich: C.H. Beck, 2002.

Pavillon, Olivier: *Des Suisses au coeur de la traité négrière: De Marseille à l'Île de France, d'Amsterdam aux Guyanes (1770–1840)*, Lausanne: Antipodes, 2017.

Purtschert, Patricia: *Kolonialität und Geschlecht im 20. Jahrhundert: Eine Geschichte der weissen Schweiz*, Bielefeld: transcript, 2019.

Purtschert, Patricia, and Harald Fischer-Tiné (eds.): *Colonial Switzerland: Rethinking Colonialism from the Margins*, Houndmills: Palgrave, 2015.

Purtschert, Patricia, Barbara Lüthi and Francesca Falk (eds.): *Postkoloniale Schweiz: Formen und Folgen eines Kolonialismus ohne Kolonie*, Bielefeld: transcript, 2012.

Veyrassat, Béatrice: *Histoire de la Suisse et des Suisses dans la marche du monde*, Neuchâtel: Livreo-Alphil, 2018.

Zangger, Andreas: *Koloniale Schweiz: Ein Stück Globalgeschichte zwischen Europa und Südostasien*, Bielefeld: transcript, 2011.

Introductions

Tracing the legacy
of colonialism
in the Swiss
National Museum

Heidi Amrein

The Swiss National Museum is one of the few cultural history museums in Switzerland without an ethnographic collection of its own. Thus, its holdings do not include objects that might have originally come from a colonial context. It is interesting that the Zurich Ethnographic Society submitted a request to the Federal Department of Home Affairs in 1893 for permission to exhibit its collection on the ground floor of the projected Swiss National Museum. The committee of the museum denied the request because the institution's scope was to be confined to Swiss history. Today, the collection of the Ethnographic Society is housed in the Ethnographic Museum at the University of Zurich.

Nevertheless, the history of the Swiss National Museum—founded by statute in 1890 and opened in 1898—contains numerous traces of colonialism, and racist or racially categorising elements and discourses can be found with respect to its events, its acquisition of objects, and its presentation of individual exhibits. Not until 2017 did exhibitions begin to focus on Switzerland's colonial entanglements.

The following remarks focus on just a few traces of the colonial heritage that can be found in the Swiss National Museum.

“Civilised people” vs. “savages”

Numerous political debates took place in the run-up to the founding of the museum, dealing with issues such as whether the Swiss federal state, founded in 1848, needed a national museum at all in addition to the various cantonal museums; options for preventing Switzerland’s cultural assets from being sold abroad; and whether the Swiss people had common ancestors.

While these discussions were in progress, archaeologists were excavating pile-dwelling settlements on many Swiss lakes. Headlines were made by the discoveries at Lake Neuenburg and Lake Biel, in which Victor Gross (1845–1920), a doctor, archaeologist, and collector with extensive international connections, played a significant role. His collection, which included human skulls, was exhibited at the world expos in Vienna in 1873 and Paris in 1878. Gross offered his collection for sale in Switzerland, but was also prepared to sell internationally if no local buyer could be found. This is where Rudolf Virchow (1821–1902) comes into play. An internationally renowned doctor, anthropologist, prehistorian, and politician, he specialised in craniometry. He founded the Berlin Anthropological Society (which would later become the Berlin Society for Anthropology, Ethnology, and Prehistory), several of whose members were in frequent contact with Swiss scholars. Virchow himself corresponded closely with Swiss colleagues as well as political figures.

He studied numerous skulls from Gross's collection, especially those from the excavations of Auvernier, and wrote a detailed preface to Gross's 1883 study *Les Protohélvètes ou les premiers colons sur les bords des lacs de Bienne et Neuchâtel,* in which he discussed the significance of his research and thus provided the young Swiss state with arguments for a shared history of origin and with reasons for purchasing the collection. He stresses that the inhabitants of the pile dwellings were a "civilised people" who, in contrast to "savages", had been capable of intellectual progress. "Unlike most savages of our time, they were not doomed to extinction as soon as the wave of civilisation reached them." Virchow here alludes to Indigenous peoples living in Europe's colonies, large numbers of whom were murdered or enslaved in the course of colonisation. During the colonial period, Indigenous peoples were portrayed as "savages" and thus perceived as inferior and backward.

An excerpt from the preface was quoted by Federal Councillor Karl Schenk (1823–1895) when, on 25 November 1884, he brought forward a motion in the Federal Assembly to purchase the Gross collection with a view to establishing a national museum in the future. "Nothing in the physical peculiarities of this race suggests an inferiority of their bodily characteristics. On the contrary, it must be acknowledged that this flesh was of our own flesh and blood. The magnificent skulls of Auvernier can be displayed with honour among the skulls of civilised peoples.

Lady of Auvernier

Julius Kollmann (1834–1918), a professor of anatomy who became rector of the University of Basel in 1888, studied the prehistoric skulls of Auvernier and used them as the basis for this reconstruction to create a kind of “primordial Swiss woman”.

Reconstruction of a prehistoric skull, 1900, Natural History Museum Basel.

Thanks to their capacity, their shape, and their physical details, they are equal to the finest skulls of the Aryan race."

Thus the core arguments in favour of purchasing the collection, which is today held by the Swiss National Museum, were based on a racist mindset ← fig. p. 28 that assumed the existence of inferior and superior "races" and distinguished between "civilised peoples" and "savages".

In the early twentieth century, the Department of Anthropology at Zurich University was internationally renowned for its global "race research". → Marilyn Umurungi p. 219 The Swiss National Museum was in close contact with the department, especially during the tenure of Otto Schlaginhaufen as director (from 1917 to 1950), who analysed the human bones excavated by the museum. The practice of categorising people into "races" persisted for many years in archaeology and was often treated on an equal footing with concepts such as ethnicity or social origins. As late as 1986, for example, the Landesmuseum Zürich put on the exhibition *Early medieval people from the perspective of anthropology and medicine*, which purported to show that people could be categorised by the size of their skulls. One display claimed that people with large skulls belonged to the nobility, while those with the smallest skulls were the unfree.

The "race" discourse is also reflected in the annual reports of the Landesmuseum. The 1905 report, for example, reads: "Such illustrated volumes [as these] are not intended as templates for the kind of slavish copying that might suppress independent, thoughtful creativity." Similar phrases also occur in the 1931 report: "Without adhering slavishly to the model, he created a charming cabinet piece." Thus the term "slavish" denotes an incapacity for independent thought and creative endeavour and is based on the conviction that, unlike "cultured"—i.e. *white*—people, enslaved people lack these qualities. This is only one example of the extent to which racist attitudes are entrenched in everyday language.

On public display

On 1 February 1913, the *Zürcher Wochenchronik* published a detailed report about a figural automaton on display in the Landesmuseum. The object in question, which was described until very recently as the "Automated M—", was a gift from the Zurich Town Council to the mayor, Hans Rudolf Rahn, in 1646 while he was staying at a health spa in Baden; today it is kept in storage at the Landesmuseum. Ever since the sixteenth century, the Rahn family crest has included the stereotypical depiction of a Black person, then termed *M—*. Tellingly, this figure was adopted by numerous wealthy families in the course of the rise of the transatlantic slave trade.

→ fig. p. 31

The following are some of the remarks from the report in the newspaper *Zürcher Wochenchronik:* "The dark gift of Baden was, in fact, a coal-black

Figure clock

The figure moves its eyes at the second and its lower jaw every hour. These kinds of exoticised depictions of Black people became increasingly popular in the wake of European expansion and colonialism.

Figure clock owned by Hans Rudolf Rahn, Augsburg, Zurich, 1646, private collection, Swiss National Museum.

Skid figure

The skid figure of this sleigh is a stereotypical representation of a half-naked Black man wearing a turban, a golden torque, and a feathered loincloth. Although resembling a neck ornament, the torque is an allusion to the collars that were used in chaining enslaved people.

Ceremonial sleigh, Thurgau, mid-18th c., Swiss National Museum.

M— made of wood. His entire droll figure was no longer than the dainty arm of a Zurich beauty who might have clapped her hands together above her bonnet in surprise and startlement." The figure is then described as "the little heathen" who "shimmers like a parrot". Also rating a mention are his "rolling eyes" and his "mouth in the most lifelike crimson with six white, tame teeth". "The manikin [...] can be seen every day in a glass case in the Schweizerisches Landesmuseum [...]. His clock ticks away in the ceremonial hall [which came] from the Lochmannhaus in Zurich [...] all should go and view the M—!"

The detailed description of the spectacle that the figure presents every second and on the hour is reminiscent of the enthusiastic reports about the "human zoos" of the time. As we mentioned above, the figural automaton was exhibited in the ceremonial hall of Oberst [Colonel] Heinrich Lochmann (1613–1667), who acquired great wealth in the service of the French and then upon his return built the chateau Langer Stadelhof; the ceremonial hall was originally located in this building.

→ Marina Amstad p.79

→ Marilyn Umurungi p.219

Depicting stereotypical Black people on objects of prestige was very popular between the mid-sixteenth and the eighteenth centuries. Half-naked Black figures, often wearing only a feathered loincloth, evoke the exotic, dark-skinned "Other" in contrast to the superior *white* identity.

← fig. p.32

This iconography of the "savage" and "exotic" also underpinned the design of the float created by the canton of Vaud at the opening ceremony of

→ fig. p.35

the Swiss National Museum in June 1898. The canton staged a wine festival with a Bacchus float led by *white* men in blackface, a practice which does not seem to have raised eyebrows in particular at the time.

Exhibition practice

Narratives about the colonial past did not find their way into exhibitions until more recent times. The 2017 exhibition devoted to Walter Mittelholzer (1894–1937), a pioneer aviator, photographer, and entrepreneur, pointed out the colonial aspect of his richly illustrated travel reports from Africa. The acquisition and analysis of a large collection of chintz fabrics copied and manufactured by numerous Swiss companies in the eighteenth and nineteenth centuries was the starting point for exhibitions at Château de Prangins in the canton of Vaud and at the Landesmuseum Zürich. The exhibitions focused on the vital function of these fabrics as bartered goods for the transatlantic trade in enslaved people. The permanent exhibition "History of Switzerland", in contrast, which opened in 2019, did not mention the colonial past until recently. For example, the life of Karl Krüsi (1855–1925), an emigrant who owned a plantation on Sumatra and became wealthy after initial setbacks, is told as a success story. To highlight the multifarious colonial references in the exhibition, numerous exhibits were

→ fig. pp. 92-95

→ Jovita dos Santos Pinto p. 97

→ Andreas Zangger p. 123

Festive procession

A wine festival organised by the canton of Vaud for the ceremonial procession to mark the opening of what is now known as the Swiss National Museum in 1898. The troupe is led by men in black make-up (a practice condemned today as “blackface”).

Waadt, Wine festival in Vivis, R. Bürgi, Festumzugsalbum Landesmuseumsfeier, Zurich, 1898, Swiss National Museum.

supplemented by texts, documents, and in some cases additional objects in 2023, and special tours on colonialism were introduced, led by experts on the subject. Texts were also expanded and adapted in the collections and the family exhibition. The texts about the figural automaton discussed above are a case in point.

Outlook

The examples discussed here show that, although the Swiss National Museum has no ethnographic collection of its own, many traces of the colonial past can nevertheless be found in its history and its exhibition practice. Examining the museum's history with a "colonial gaze" and "decolonising" the museum: what does that mean? What does a given object tell us, and how can we draw out, reconstruct, and communicate hitherto hidden histories and make them accessible for the future? Both the reappraisal of the collection and its inventory in the object database and the present exhibition are contributions to a process that is only just beginning.

Byston, Daniela, and Anne Fäser (eds.): *Das Museum dekolonisieren? Kolonialität und museale Praxis in Berlin,* Bielefeld: transcript, 2022.

Meier, Joschka: "Eugenik, Rassentheorie und völkische Ideologie: Zwei Beiträge zur Rolle der schweizerischen Forschung", in *Bern Working Papers on Prehistoric Archaeology,* no. 4, part 1, Bern: Institut für Archäologische Wissenschaft, Prähistorische Archäologie/Universität Bern, 2022, pp. 5–22.

Soares, Bruno Brulon, and Andrea Witcomb: "Towards Decolonisation" in *Museum International*, 74/3–4, 2022: www.tandfonline.com/toc/rmil20/74/3-4?nav=tocList (accessed 29 Sep. 2023).

Overdue attention

How the Swiss role in European colonialism was discovered

Georg Kreis

As we all know, history is a broad field. There is no doctrine that tells us what to explore, how, when, and why, and what areas should be called to mind with the aid of temporary museum exhibitions. Based on a handful of examples, this essay shows that the historiography of Switzerland's colonial involvement was conditioned by the times in which it was written and asks why the transnational dimensions of Switzerland's history were ignored in the past and are only now being reappraised.

Different periods elicit different perspectives on history. Even the Third World movement, which arose in the 1960s, saw no need to criticise the lack of analysis of Switzerland's role in colonial regimes. The movement's commitment, arising from an acute awareness of the material needs of the "Third World", was decidedly focused on the present and future, with little regard for the past. After the turn of the millennium, however, Switzerland's focus on its colonial past took a different turn, both in terms of quantity as well as quality: quantitatively, in that the subject of the colonial past was brought up much more frequently; and qualitatively, in that research increasingly adopted a postcolonial stance that was met with remarkably widespread acceptance. As far as Switzerland is concerned, the postcolonial debate has thus far brought into focus criticism that the role the country played in the spread of European colonialism had been repressed and that, as a result, its impact on modern Swiss society had been largely ignored, and that it is therefore now the task of historians to start dealing in earnest with the country's colonial past.

Rise of the postcolonial paradigm

For some time now, the new paradigm of postcolonialism has been present in a way that makes the question of when and how it arose appear superfluous. Just how did the colonial past become such a key topic of study and lead to this new academic turn? A common method of answering this question from the perspective of the history of ideas is to identify ground-breaking authors who provided important stimulus for further study. However, the literature rightly points out that there is no such "point zero" in the field of postcolonial study.[1] Nevertheless, the Palestinian-American literary scholar Eduard Said's 1978 book *Orientalism* is today considered a kind of "founding document".[2]

Another strategy seeks explanations for the rise of postcolonialism in the reigning social conditions and attitudes and assumes that these are what determine the course of academic research. Many combined factors can be brought into play here: globalisation, which is bringing the world's regions closer together; increased migration from the Global South to the Global North; and the tendency to focus more intently on the fate of victims and the liability of perpetrators; addressing discrimination, both past and present, in conjunction with demands for justice and recompense in various forms. Broaching these matters has undoubtedly also benefited from the fact that increasing numbers of people of non-European origin now live among us and that their voices and writings now receive more public recognition. The press portraits of the Cameroonian historian Olivette Otele, who teaches in the UK, and of the Indian historian Debjani Bhattacharyya, who teaches in Switzerland, are just two examples in this vein.

The World Conference against Racism, Racial Discrimination, Xenophobia and Related Intolerance held in Durban in the autumn of 2001 provided an important impetus in dealing with the colonial past. When asked how Switzerland should respond to calls for reparations for the colonial past and the trade in enslaved people, one of the official Swiss representatives, Jean-Daniel Vigny, adopted a typically Swiss stance. He argued that this was a conflict involving industrial nations and developing countries, but considering that Switzerland had never been directly involved in the matter, they would be happy to serve as mediators. He saw no reason for Switzerland to become involved in the issue of reparations since the country "had never had anything to do with slavery, the slave trade, and colonialism". In saying so, he utterly neglected the fact that the country certainly did have "something to do" with the issue, given the involvement of Swiss actors in colonial enterprises, their role in the colonial slave economy and as mercenaries in colonial territories, or their part in Christian proselytisation in Africa and India.

The widely spread perception, which ignores or overlooks the activities of private Swiss citizens in colonial regions and in the trade with enslaved people and which claims a special status for Switzerland separate from the rest of the world despite the country's global foreign entanglements, was subsequently viewed by critics as a crucial statement and taken as welcome proof of the prevalence of a flawed view of history that suppressed the grave realities. Shortly after the Durban conference, additional, important ideas for intensifying the engagement with the colonial past were put forward by the historian and teacher Hans Fässler from St Gallen.[3] At his incentive, a number of political initiatives were launched at the federal level and within the cantons that sought to address this hitherto neglected aspect of Swiss history.

In Switzerland, it is probably no coincidence that women have played a leading role in drawing attention to postcolonialism. The analysis of postcolonial Switzerland put forward by Patricia Purtschert, Barbara Lüthi, and Francesca Falk in 2012 received a great deal of attention.[4] Its authors presented a "different view" and a "new field of discussion", although they acknowledged that their postcolonial interest did "not primarily" focus on the economic dimensions of Swiss colonial involvement, but rather on "the cultural aspects of colonialism (and, thus, the discursive, semantic, and imaginary moulding of colonial projects)". They avoided using the term "guilt", focusing instead on "complicity" (in quotation marks). What remains unanswered, however, is how colonial participation should be described and whether Swiss individuals involved in colonial projects should be described as henchmen, accessories, collaborators, profiteers, freeloaders, or accomplices. Their remarks suggest that the focus on postcolonialism merely represents a variant of a more general critique of the same prevailing power relations that underpin the overlapping and mutually reinforcing issues of sexism, homophobia, and class conflict—practices that often tend to crosscut boundaries and occur in combination. Purtschert devoted further essays to this additional aspect a few years later.

The concept of postcolonialism thus introduced into Swiss historiography was generally welcomed by academic peers. The contribution made in 2010 by Harald Fischer-Tiné, a lecturer in history at ETH Zürich, offers the most in-depth and clear interpretation of this new research paradigm. Fischer-Tiné does not perceive colonialism as a closed historical episode; the prefix "post" in postcolonial is not to be taken temporally as meaning "after colonialism", but should be understood as a postulate of a current engagement with and a future overcoming of colonial premises. However, Fischer-Tiné also noted that "in this general criticism of power, the concrete relationship with the historical phenomenon of European colonialism is sometimes barely recognisable".[5] From the post-colonial perspective, the question of the effects of colonialism on colonised regions/societies/people during and in the aftermath of the colonial era is, indeed, notably absent. Here the commendable self-critical stance appears first and foremost as a new but negative version of Eurocentrism.

Andreas Zangger's dissertation (2011) on colonial Switzerland holds a special position in the literature in two respects: firstly, it examines Swiss participation in European colonialism in the Asian and not in the African sphere, as does Bernhard C. Schär's monograph published in 2015.[6] Secondly, it is not confined to a Eurocentric view of colonial actors, but also briefly examines the effects of colonial activities on the colonised population. Zangger introduces the term *Beteiligungsgeschichte* (participation history) and draws obvious parallels with the discussions surrounding Swiss "involvement" in the Third Reich that dominated Swiss historical scholarship during the 1990s.[7]

The increased interest in Switzerland's role in colonial history is a variant of efforts that can also be observed in other national histories, which seek to take transnational realities into account when examining national issues. In Switzerland, André Holenstein's 2014 book *Mitten in Europa. Verflechtung und Abgrenzung in der Schweizer Geschichte* (In the Centre of Europe: Entanglement and Disassociation in Swiss History) arose from this new focus on “entanglement” as a reaction to the challenges at the level of European policymaking. The title of his book could easily be extended to include *In the Centre of the World.*

The fact that Switzerland’s involvement in European colonialism was ignored for a long time played into the assumption that, at this level too, the small country stands outside the wider European history, occupying a special status, which allows it to regard itself as an innocent country and which obviates any need to examine the extent to which it might bear responsibility for events that happened beyond its borders. The sensitivity to these issues that has developed in recent years, however, means that the entanglements of Swiss protagonists with the “rest of the world” are now perceived more clearly and that, more specifically, their role in European colonialism has now been “revealed”. What has also been discovered is the large number of studies published on the subject, not all of which can be listed here.[8] These and other studies have prepared the ground for the exhibition and accompanying catalogue *colonial—Switzerland’s Global Entanglements* at the Swiss National Museum.

1 Varela, Castro, María do Mar, and Nikita Dhawan: *Postkoloniale Theorie: Eine kritische Einführung*, 3rd ed., Bielefeld: transcript, 2020, pp. 99–159.

2 Said, Edward W.: *Orientalism*, New York: Pantheon, 1978.

3 Fässler, Hans: *Reise in Schwarz-Weiss: Schweizer Ortstermine in Sachen Sklaverei*, Zurich: Rotpunktverlag, 2005.

4 Purtschert, Patricia, Barbara Lüthi, and Francesca Falk (eds.): *Postkoloniale Schweiz: Formen und Folgen eines Kolonialismus ohne Kolonien,* Bielefeld: transcript, 2012, pp. 13–63.

5 Fischer-Tiné, Harald: *Postkoloniale Studien,* Europäische Geschichte Online [website], 2010, http://ieg-ego.eu/de/threads/europa-und-die-welt/postkoloniale-studien (accessed 13 Dec. 2023).

6 Schär, Bernhard C.: *Tropenliebe: Schweizer Naturforscher und niederländischer Imperialismus in Südostasien um 1900,* Frankfurt am Main: Campus, 2015.

7 Zangger, Andreas: *Koloniale Schweiz: Ein Stück Globalgeschichte zwischen Europa und Südostasien (1860–1930),* Bielefeld: transcript, 2011.

8 Kreis, Georg: *Blicke auf die koloniale Schweiz: Ein Forschungsbericht,* Zurich: Chronos, 2023.

Divisive and unifying

Colonial history for a just future

Monique Ligtenberg
Bernhard C. Schär

In 2021, Swiss banks managed roughly 22 per cent of the world's cross-border assets, while in the same year Swiss companies employed around 2.1 million people abroad—over half of them outside Europe. With its foreign investments, Switzerland consistently ranks among the world's ten leading countries. Whether tea, coffee, Ovaltine, or orange juice, almost everyone living in Switzerland starts their day with a beverage whose raw materials are produced in the "Global South" under precarious working conditions and for low wages.

This is not the only downside of Switzerland's remarkable globality. According to sociological studies, around 25 per cent of Swiss people harbour xenophobic beliefs, and ten per cent of these are openly racist. The result is that many residents of Switzerland are confronted with racist discrimination in the work and housing market, based on their skin colour, religion, or country of origin.

Migration, global prosperity gaps, and racism all have one thing in common: they are partly the result of the European conquests that took place between approximately 1500 and the second half of the twentieth century. Switzerland was always a key player in these global events and never stood on the sidelines. However, the question of whether Switzerland played a role in, and was shaped by, European expansion has long been neglected by historians. Even in the Swiss National Museum, examinations of colonial history have been little more than side notes.

Swiss history and "colonial amnesia"

Not that Switzerland was an exception in ignoring its own colonial history; indeed, this has been normal European practice, and it was not until recently that other European countries began exploring their own colonial pasts. Experts in the field also refer to this state of affairs as "colonial amnesia". It has influenced European and Swiss history in two ways. First, Swiss narratives are all too often bound up with a nationalistic discourse that highlights the country's economic success in order to strengthen a national sense of identity. One aspect of this success story is a phenomenon the Dutch cultural scientist Gloria Wekker has described as "White innocence", that is to say, the idea that Switzerland has remained untouched in both past and present by the effects of colonial violence and racial discrimination. The second trait of this colonial amnesia is Eurocentrism—in other words, the assumption that only what happens in a supposedly "civilised" Europe is worthy of discussion and that the history of Switzerland can therefore only be understood when it is examined within a Western European/North Atlantic context. For the most part, this belief has led historians to ignore the knowledge and actions of non-European regions and peoples in the historical development of Switzerland, thus rendering them virtually invisible.

The concepts of Eurocentrism and "White innocence" remained uncontested for as long as Swiss history was written almost exclusively by *white* Christian authors, most of them male, for a peer audience. For a long time, they had no need to address the perspectives of voiceless "foreigners" living in the country—not to mention those living abroad. But this power relationship has shifted in recent times. Ever larger segments of the Swiss population are now criticising these narratives as being contradictory to their daily reality, which is characterised by racism and other forms of discrimination, and are now developing their own narratives within the context of postcolonial theatres, exhibitions, podcasts, podia, public demonstrations, blogs, and city tours.

This shift found its way into the country's universities and colleges through the work of undergraduate and graduate students and has been met with keen interest by specialists in non-European history as well as students in disciplines such as urban and gender studies. Their efforts have resulted in a new interdisciplinary field of research known as "postcolonial Switzerland", which is gradually making it possible to discuss Swiss history as something other than merely a part of European history, supposedly untouched by colonial expansion. As a result, Swiss history is increasingly being understood as a history of relationships that developed within a global framework and in constant, albeit hierarchical and often violent, contact with people on all continents of the world.

The exhibition at the National Museum Zurich palpably illustrates the far-reaching consequences of these developments. Rather than merely supplementing traditional accounts of Swiss history with these previously neglected aspects, a postcolonial history of Switzerland also offers new perspectives for looking at colonial history in general.

Colonial Switzerland?

The German historians Jürgen Osterhammel and Joël Glasmann have offered helpful definitions of the phenomenon known as "colonialism", describing it as rule by a foreign minority that is unwilling to adapt over societies beyond their own region of origin. In the case of European colonialism, what is at issue is the relationship of domination between European centres of power and regions on all other continents. One main characteristic of this form of rule is a dual legal system which attributes privileges to Europeans on the basis of their skin colour and ascribes only instrumental value to all others, who are referred to as "natives" *(indigènes, indígenas)* or "creoles" *(mixed race, mestizos, métissés)* and regarded as nothing but a labour force for European profit and as peoples to be Christianised and Europeanised. Indeed, Switzerland as a nation was never involved in colonialism on this scale. Never in its history did the country rule over large stretches of Asia, Africa, or the Americas.

It is only when we adopt a view of colonial history that transcends this nation-state perspective that we can begin to grasp Switzerland's role in the colonial world. Firstly, European colonial powers required large armies to secure their rule over the long term. From the early modern period up until the twentieth century, Swiss men served these European colonial powers as mercenaries. In doing so, they participated in a system of violence that was an integral aspect of colonial rule, since people who resisted were met with either active or passive annihilation almost everywhere. The best-known examples are the extermination of nearly 90 per cent of the indigenous population of the Americas as a result of violence and introduced diseases; the genocide that took place on the Dutch-conquered Banda Islands in South-East Asia in 1621; the eradication of the population of Tasmania in the South Pacific in the nineteenth century; and the genocide of the Herero and Nama in former German South West Africa, now Namibia, from 1904 to 1908. Thousands of Swiss men serving as soldiers and officers in the Dutch and British East India Companies, in the French Foreign Legion in North Africa and South-East Asia, and in the Dutch colonial army in Indonesia were directly involved in such colonial acts of violence.

Secondly, the colonial conquest of the world went hand in hand with the establishment of a global economic system that was open to individuals and companies from regions that did not maintain colonies of their own. The roots of this economic process of globalisation can be traced back to the transatlantic slave trade, which resulted in more than twelve million people being transported from the African continent to the Americas. The trading companies responsible for these abductions were co-financed by Swiss investors. Even after the abolishment of slavery, Swiss merchants and plantation owners continued to profit from the trade in raw materials produced under exploitative conditions.

Thirdly, the colonial powers resorted to a system of thought that predicated a hierarchy between "superior Europeans" and the "uncivilised rest of the world" to provide moral legitimacy for violence and economic exploitation. It must be stressed here that colonialism was not built upon pre-existing ethnic, cultural, religious, or other differences; such differences were invented or at least radically accentuated by the colonial powers. Convinced that non-Christian forms of spirituality were "barbaric", Swiss missionaries travelled to the European colonies, where they sought to "convert" the "heathens" to the supposedly superior religion of Christianity. Through the influence of travel reports, advertising, and school textbooks, claims of Christian, European, and *white* superiority found their way into everyday Swiss culture. Swiss universities and museums also played an important role in the quest to prove the existence of different human "races", and, in doing, so they supplied a supposedly scientific legitimation of colonial rule. Thus, colonialism represented a mechanism that constantly constructed differences and sorted people into categories, the after-effects of which continue to shape numerous religious and ethnic conflicts to this day.

In short, colonialism displayed a number of dimensions, and Switzerland avoided playing a direct role in only one of these—the political dimension. All the others, from trade and financing through emigration and missionary work to scientific theory and everyday culture, were shaped with Switzerland's participation and exercised a lasting influence on the country in turn.

The reason for Switzerland's significant presence in "foreign" colonies is relatively simple. European colonies were all rather large in size. Since colonial powers such as Great Britain, France, Portugal, the Netherlands, and Belgium were quite small by comparison, they lacked the financial, military, technical, and other resources to develop a colonial empire, nor did they have a large enough labour force in their own countries for the purpose. Therefore, all the imperial powers were reliant in one way or another on neighbouring European states for capital, settlers, soldiers, missionaries, researchers, etc. This lasting demand enabled European regions which would only later—or not at all—develop their own overseas empires to share in the colonial projects of their European neighbours. Swiss active overseas were thus never simply the henchmen of the established colonial powers. They were following their own financial, religious, or scientific interests. In the case of missionaries, however, their work could lead to conflicts with the colonial powers, which feared that proselytising might provoke revolts among native populations.

Furthermore, Switzerland's "colonialism without colonies" was not unique. Countries such as Finland, Hungary, and Poland were also involved in colonial projects. But countries such as Germany, Italy, and Belgium, which were relatively slow to establish colonial empires, had been participating in the imperial projects of other nations for centuries. Thus, Switzerland was part of a larger European pool of resources, services, and personnel for the colonial projects of other great imperial powers.

This had far-reaching consequences both for the colonies themselves and for Switzerland, as the essays collected in this volume show. We will conclude here by examining why the historical awareness of Switzerland's past colonial entanglements is relevant to our crisis-ridden, globalised present.

Divided history(-ies)

The extent to which domestic technological innovation and overseas colonial exploitation played a role in the development of European wealth is a controversial topic of debate among economic historians. What is certain, however, is that Switzerland belonged to the group of European regions that experienced the highest level of economic growth during the colonial era. To date, however, we have very little understanding of what this meant for the countless individuals around the world who were involved in these developments, and how their descendants are still affected by them to this day. Recent research has also shown that it is important to differentiate: racism and lasting inequality between the Global North and South are a fundamental part of the story. Neither European nor the colonised societies were homogeneous, however. Rather, they were often characterised by a number of internal hierarchies. Apart from violence and exploitation, Europe's colonial expansion also brought with it a range of opportunities and risks on both sides, although it was primarily the Europeans who benefited in the long run. This is why examinations of specific circumstances are just as important as general studies of colonial development.

We know of numerous examples of Asian, African, and Latin American elites who collaborated with European colonial powers and, in doing so, ensured their own prosperity and political influence. This came at the expense of a majority of the population, which to this day continues to suffer from the social and economic divides established and reinforced under colonial rule. Switzerland played a conspicuous role in small but often very influential areas, as Isabelle Lucas has shown in the case of the Swiss electricity industry in Argentina.

On the Swiss side too, however, the "profits" from colonialism warrant a nuanced examination. For example, as the contribution by Philipp Krauer

→ Philipp Krauer p. 143

shows, most of the Swiss mercenaries who served in colonial armies did not share in the wealth that their violent actions in the service of the colonial powers enabled and protected. Around half of them died of diseases or in armed conflicts. Those who survived received a modest veteran's pension that was typically used to support parents, siblings, and families also living in precarious conditions. Switzerland's economic growth during the colonial era also perpetuated significant social disparity among Swiss people at home.

Wealth and inequality affected women and men in very different ways. As is well known, Swiss women were effectively disenfranchised until the 1970s and thus enjoyed fewer rights in their own country than women in Latin American, South Asian, or West African countries that had gained independence. For women of the upper classes, however, colonialism provided greater latitude for action. Their involvement in a Christian mission, for example, often opened up economic opportunities and freedoms that they would have been denied in Switzerland. During the colonial era, poor women and men in Switzerland were often subjected to a regime of "compulsory social measures". Thousands of "indolent" men and "wanton" women were consigned to institutions, and their children were sent to work or placed in homes or foster families, where they were often subjected to psychological and sexual abuse. It is estimated that several hundred thousand Swiss were affected by such actions, including the small Yenish minority. These segments of Swiss society were not among the beneficiaries of European colonialism, nor is it an accident that their fates closely resemble those of indigenous societies in *white* settler colonies, as the research of Manuel Menrath has shown. Large numbers of indigenous children in the United States and Canada were forcibly separated from their parents and placed in boarding schools, where the "I—" were to be raised to become "moral people". One of the most influential individuals involved in this re-education programme in the United States was the "I— missionary" Martin Marty from the Canton of Schwyz.

For almost five hundred years, European rule in the colonies as well as in Europe itself was based on interwoven forms of exploitation and violence according to categories such as "race", religion, gender, and social status. The future will certainly not be less globally linked than the past. If this future is to be well-informed, democratic, and liveable for coming generations, it is important that a transnationally linked society such as Switzerland be aware of the extent to which racist stereotypes as well as social and economic disparities from the colonial era still haunt us today. This includes the question of how we can overcome the social divides based on origin, religion, skin colour, sexual orientation, and gender, which were established during the colonial era and still represent obstacles to empathy and solidarity between people.

The colonial past
in Switzerland's
collective memory

Hannan Salamat

In 2023, the exhibition *Blind Spots: Zurich and Colonialism* ("Blinde Flecken – Zürich und der Kolonialismus") was shown at the Stadthaus in Zurich. This elaborate exhibition, which was accompanied by an extensive supporting programme featuring a wide range of voices, shed light on Zurich's entanglements with colonial history. An increasing number of Swiss cities and communities are now beginning to focus on this issue, as intensive research carried out over the past two decades has irrefutably shown that Switzerland—although it had no colonies of its own—was involved in colonialism in a number of ways, be it through its role in the trade in enslaved people and raw materials or through missionary work. Still, most Swiss have very little knowledge of this history, or none at all. How is that possible? The lack of knowledge can be explained by the fact that this history is insufficiently anchored in the country's collective memory. And this public blank spot has consequences which, today, become manifest in the form of individual, institutional, and structural racism. Upon closer inspection, it becomes clear that other histories of violence also receive little attention. In examining how these blank spots came about, I believe it is important to examine the concept of neutrality in the context of the Swiss culture of remembrance. This essay will briefly outline the origins of these blank spots and how they relate to the narrative of a neutral Switzerland.

What is remembrance?

For many years I have been engaging intensely with the "culture of remembrance". Ever since moving to Switzerland in 2017, I have sought to determine the exact mechanisms that define remembrance in this country. During a panel discussion at the Stadthaus in Zurich in 2021 marking the fiftieth anniversary of women's suffrage, my use of the term "culture of remembrance" was a source of confusion, as many participants immediately associated the term with the German historical reappraisal of the Nazi era. Had I imported a German term? In the autumn of that same year, however, Switzerland's culture of remembrance drew worldwide attention when an extension was added to the Kunsthaus Zürich to house, among other works, the collection belonging to Emil Bührle, a weapons manufacturer. Bührle's dealings with Nazi Germany made him the richest man in Switzerland in the 1930s. His art collection included works that had been stolen from Jewish collectors or were purchased from people forced to sell owing to Nazi persecution. These individuals, however, were hardly mentioned in the exhibition. Although the city of Zurich aimed to bolster its international reputation with this exhibition, in the end it drew only derision. Journalists from New York to Berlin shook their heads in dismay. Many asked how such a fraught legacy could be presented in such a thoughtless manner after the release of the Bergier Report by the Independent Commission of Experts (UEK) in 2002, which offered a thorough reappraisal of Swiss culpability and shared responsibility during the Second World War. In addition, the historian Thomas Buomberger and art historian Guido Magnaguagno published a detailed examination of Emil Bührle and his problematic collection in 2015.

Forgetting is closely connected with remembering. Memories do not offer an objective portrayal of the past, and collective memory more properly reflects how history impacts the present. The culture of remembrance can thus be viewed as the way in which a society, in the present, deals with its own past and can give rise to widely differing interpretations and elaborations, depending on the recipients. Furthermore, the existence of plural realities mean that more than one culture of remembrance can exist within a society. This plurality also shows how cultural practices of remembrance are dynamic and seek to fulfil the desire for community, exoneration, continuity, and identification with a particular concept of the self and the environment. Memories are also not neutral; they are coloured by the perspectives of those who shape the hegemonial historical narrative. Cultures of remembrance can thus choose to make visible the needs, experiences, and perspectives of particular groups, while inevitably excluding others. In this process, elements such as resources, for example, state funding for exhibitions or decisions regarding monuments or commemoration days, are critical in determining what is anchored in the collective memory and who determines the interpretation of the present—and, in so doing, shapes the vision of the future. Whatever does not serve a positive self-image of the dominant culture is often consigned to oblivion. All these factors ensure that cultures of remembrance are political struggles that fight to determine how a society narrates itself: those whose perspective carries the most weight are the ones who decide who is perceived as "us" in society, and who is excluded.

What is neutrality?

When I ask people in Switzerland to describe the factors that determine the country's self-image, neutrality is one of the first things to be mentioned. Most of them, however, are not referring to the core legal definition whereby neutral states do not get involved in wars between other countries. This aspect also applies to other neutral nations, such as Austria. Still, the perception of neutrality differs significantly in Switzerland and Austria, particularly regarding its political dimension, which functions as a key element in Switzerland's collective self-image. The idea that neutrality is a part of the Swiss identity is deeply rooted in history. As early as 1943, the historian Edgar Bonjour described Swiss neutrality as a "national myth of almost religious sanctity". Of course, this narrative is no longer regarded as unquestionable and has been discussed in dozens of papers. Particularly since the beginning of the Russian war of aggression in Ukraine in February 2022, acceptance of neutrality has been in decline. According to an ETH survey, however, Swiss neutrality was still regarded as a significant aspect of the country's identity in 2023.

In this self-image of a neutral state, the country appears as a harmonious, idyllic place, and this image colours public debate about social deficits. This has consequences. In the context of the culture of remembrance, neutrality serves as a filter in that, while public discussions do focus on the violent aspects of Swiss history, they still refrain from questioning or seeking to change existing power relationships in the present. In the context of Germany, the author Max Czollek describes this process as the "theatre of reconciliation", the creation of a new self-image for the German population marked by catharsis and rectification thanks to the public culture of remembrance. This German theatre of reconciliation is in many ways different from the Swiss narrative of neutrality. Neutrality functions on a more subtle level, like an invisible curtain that transforms the act of self-reflection into an illusion of idyll and harmony. One could also interpret this as the conscious repression of any kind of critical faculty. In order to make this nuanced mechanism more tangible, I would like to term this process the "neutrality theatre", as, notwithstanding the differences between the two cases, the elements of theatre are present in many aspects of both.

In the course of my work, I have noticed that an analysis of this neutrality analysis uncovers a number of mechanisms that marginalised people in Switzerland have experienced for many years. It appears that this approach provides many people committed to fighting discrimination in Swiss society with an appropriate language for making visible what was previously hidden. Perhaps it is also merely an appropriate working title for a research paper aimed at describing the phases of the Swiss culture of remembrance in the recent past. But I also believe that we need a multi-perspectival analysis of the history of neutrality itself—a history which to date has mostly been one-sided.

People affected by discrimination play a particular role in the self-presentation of Switzerland as a place of idyllic harmony. In my work with Jewish, Muslim, Black, and post-migrant communities, I often sense a tendency towards inner resistance against the prevailing dominant culture. The myth of economic achievement and belonging achieved through assimilation has been so thoroughly internalised that many believe the causes for discrimination lie within themselves. I often hear Muslims says that anti-Muslim racism would not exist if they would only be "better" Muslims. This narrative reflects the adoption of stereotypes relating to the perceived threat people of Islamic faith pose to Switzerland, a country which has accepted two referendums over the last fifteen years expressing a hostile position towards Muslims.

Minorities that have internalised individual failure as a source of discrimination mirror existing social realities in the country. These strategies can be interpreted as the continuation of colonial patterns of thought and notions of cultural hierarchy. The self-ascription of blame and the desire to assimilate are signs of how deeply colonial notions of superiority and inferiority are anchored in social structures.

Der Sommer, in dem ich Schwarz wurde ("The summer I turned Black") is the title of a book by the SRF presenter Angélique Beldner, and many young Black people in Switzerland with whom I have spoken use the same formulation to refer to the summer of the Black Lives Matter (BLM) movement in 2020. Beldner describes how she had long found it inconceivable for her to speak openly about racism—not because she had never experienced it, but because she did not want her identity to play a part in her life. So, she remained silent, made allowances for racist remarks, and tried to avoid the pain—strategies I have encountered among marginalised people from a wide range of communities with which they seek to emerge untouched from experiences of violence, to protect themselves from further discrimination, to avoid standing out, and to not disturb the harmony of Switzerland. These strategies may work in the short run, but they neither reveal the social relationships involving colonial continuities, nor do they solve them. Fear of identity conflicts or negative consequences is one result of violent experiences that are anchored in all aspects of society.

As mentioned above, a society's self-narrative also determines who is perceived as "us". To this day, people who deviate from the concept of the Swiss "we" are pushed into marginal roles in order to protect the myth of a homogeneous society. The people marked as "other" or "foreign" may change over time, but their function as a projection screen for everything non-Swiss remains. Whether Italian migrant workers, asylum seekers, or Muslims, the roles may change, but the problem of marginalisation in public discourse remains the same. Black people, People of Colour, and people with a migration background continue to face discrimination. What cannot be denied, however, is that Switzerland's past and present is influenced by diversity. However, this also means that the culture of remembrance must be a pluralistic project.

What is plurality?

The global BLM movement of the summer of 2020 brought the discourse surrounding the remembrance of slavery and colonialism into focus in Switzerland. The protests coincided with the fiftieth anniversary marking the rejection of the "Schwarzenbach Initiative". One of the most prominent of numerous initiatives against excessive immigration introduced between 1968 and 2020, the aim of this campaign, launched by the right-wing populist James Schwarzenbach, was to deport up to 400,000 people, most of them Italians. The social anthropologist Rohit Jain describes the Schwarzenbach Initiative as the tip of an iceberg that revealed the contradictory nature of a racist state system in which migrant workers helped the Swiss middle class to accumulate wealth, even though they were never recognised as a part of society. In Jain's view, a culture of remembrance placing Schwarzenbach at its centre would repeat the same false analysis, according to which right-wing populism is the main problem, and divert attention away from the responsibility borne by mainstream society as well as the institutions that maintain it. In this model, "xenophobia" is often described as public irrationality stirred up by right-wing populism. According to Jain, this serves to absolve wider society of structural racism. During the BLM summer, the spotlight was quickly aimed at the question of whether racism even exists here in Switzerland, instead of focusing on the structures of racism in society and, in particular, the role of institutions in this context. Institutions are not just empty vessels; they play an important role in society and can either maintain the status quo or play an active role in coming to terms with disparities. In my work with institutions, I have noticed how self-reflection often descends into a kind of self-dramatisation. Problematic patterns of behaviour are corrected—sometimes only in response to social pressure—and this process is staged as a form of enlightened self-correction aimed at preserving a positive image. This leads, however, to the impression that there is no need for action, particularly when it comes to deeper examination that could lead to changes in existing power structures.

Cultures of remembrance transform memory into learning experiences. Nevertheless, experience alone does not necessarily mean that our societies are becoming more just. Acknowledging the need to reappraise history implies that memory must become a component of a present-day healing process.

Recognition of a plurality of cultures of remembrance shows us that the Swiss narrative to date has not included everyone. Maintaining a plurality of cultures of remembrance means ending colonial continuities—disrupting them in order to change them.

Plural cultures of remembrance mean the end of the theatre of neutrality in order to enable an honest examination of social deficits and to question our often-idealised harmonious self-image. Who profits from the narrative of a neutral Switzerland? For whom does this narrative continue to serve as a source of violence?

Plural cultures of remembrance are dynamic and are constantly developing with the aim of forming a society fit for the future, a society which includes all its members and recognises a diversity of perspectives.

Plurality is not a challenge; it is the foundation of a democratic society. What is more, it is a social reality. Plural cultures of remembrance create spaces for encounters, development, and formation in a society that is marked by differences. This is something that benefits us all.

Essays

Colonial traces
in everyday life in Switzerland

Marina Amstad

For a long time, Switzerland was a relatively poor country with a small bourgeois upper class. While many citizens and private enterprises benefited from colonial structures in various ways, most of the profits reaped directly from the colonial territories ended up in the pockets of a small elite. It was this elite that was able to operate globally through diverse international networks and that became involved in colonialism outside Switzerland. The majority of the Swiss population, on the other hand, remained rural until well into the nineteenth century—the share of the total workforce employed in agriculture was still more than 50 per cent around 1850. Most citizens suffered from poverty and did not have the opportunity to engage in colonial business. Poverty continued to be widespread in the countryside until the second half of the nineteenth century; for centuries, many Swiss people were forced to leave their homeland for economic reasons. It was not until the 1880s that Switzerland changed from an emigration to an immigration country.

Only the well-off could afford to make international investments, such as in the trade with enslaved people, or to acquire plantations in colonial territories. In those days, travel—whether for private or research purposes—was another preserve of the upper classes. But besides the bourgeois elite, it was also mercenaries, emigrants driven by poverty, and missionaries who were able to benefit from colonial structures, not only in practical terms—for example, through the transportation system—but also on account of their being European at a time of European domination. While Switzerland as a state was not involved in colonialism as such—unlike some of its individual citizens—the people of Switzerland as a whole were nonetheless influenced by colonialism.

Colonial products

The influence of colonialism on everyday life was clearly evident from the availability of imported colonial goods, which significantly changed the consumption habits of the Swiss people. The exploitation of enslaved people on plantations in the Caribbean and the Americas meant that products such as sugar, tobacco, coffee, cocoa, and spices now became affordable to others than just the economic elite. → fig. p.140 For example, coffee replaced milk soup in the eighteenth century and became popular in the nineteenth century. The beverage was essential for cottage workers, in particular, because, on the one hand, its stimulative effect made the monotonous work easier to bear but, on the other, it allowed workers to toil for longer hours. Colonial traces are evident, too, in the Swiss national dish *Rösti:* without colonialism, the potato might never have arrived in the country. It is thought that Spanish sailors brought the first specimens from South America to Europe as early as 1560, but it was not until the eighteenth century that the vegetable was cultivated as an everyday food product and thereby helped feed the rapidly growing working class during the age of industrialisation. The potato went on to become a Swiss staple food and is now perceived as a native crop. Another supposedly indigenous plant with a colonial background is the geranium—a wildflower that originally comes from South Africa and reached Switzerland in 1715 via the botanical gardens of the Dutch colonial power. Today, it adorns almost every chalet and, just like *Rösti*, epitomises home for many Swiss people. But probably the best-known product that is now seen, both nationally and internationally, as part of Swiss identity, is chocolate: without cocoa beans and sugar—both colonial products—the development of the chocolate industry in Switzerland would have been unthinkable.

In material terms, however, it was not only raw goods and products from the colonies that changed life in Switzerland; the direct flow of money played a role as well. The families and private individuals who had achieved great wealth through doing business in the colonies of the European powers often invested their profits in Switzerland, which led to the creation of numerous jobs. At the same time, they built stately homes as well as museums and hospitals. Jacques-Louis de Pourtalès (1722–1814) from Neuchâtel, for example, founded the company Pourtalès & Cie, which traded in both

Europe and the colonies and owned numerous factories for the production of chintz. These printed cotton fabrics were the most important barter goods in the slave trade, and a significant share was produced by the Swiss cotton industry. As the owner of a chintz empire, Pourtalès not only provided work for a large number of people at his factories; he also made enormous profits from the sale of the fabrics, which were intended, among other things, to be exchanged for enslaved people. In addition, Pourtalès owned plantations in the Antilles, where, with the help of hundreds of enslaved people, he grew mainly sugar beet, alongside coffee, cocoa, and cotton. In 1799, Pourtalès was probably the richest man in Switzerland. In 1808, he funded the establishment of the "Hôpital Pourtalès", a medical facility for the poor, in his hometown of Neuchâtel. Meanwhile, the families of mercenaries, often living in poverty, remained dependent on the pensions, gratuities, and estate payments that were sent from the colonies to the municipalities in Switzerland.

Colonial worldview

Situated in the middle of Europe, Switzerland is closely intertwined with other countries. After its founding, it identified itself as part of progressive Europe, allegedly superior to the rest of the world. But where does this world view come from? Here, an important role was played by the experiences of Swiss people in the colonial territories, such as missionaries, mercenaries, and emigrants. As *whites* operating in the sphere of European colonial rule, they conveyed this narrative to Switzerland through letters and reports, thereby also fuelling enthusiasm for the "exotic" and the "Other". Swiss emigration journals, such as the newspaper *Der Kolonist*, published from 1851 to 1857, conveyed the image of paradisiacal conditions in the colonies and reinforced a racist view of the indigenous population of the Americas. Literary portrayals of mercenaries and foreign legionnaires in the form of (sometimes fictitious) reports and memoirs met with huge interest in Switzerland. In these works, the inhabitants of Africa and Asia were largely portrayed as anonymous collectives and often described as "inferior" or "primitive". The experiences of Swiss missionaries drew attention particularly at church services and in religion classes, while missionary journals helped to spread the image of a "backward" Africa that needed "saving" in Swiss households.

→ Claudia Buess p.159

As the consumer society slowly emerged in Switzerland in the nineteenth century and the mass distribution of printed materials got under way, more and more products were promoted. The emerging advertising industry developed a visual language, particularly for "exotic" luxury foods such as chocolate, which relied on stereotypes of non-European people and must be classified as racist. Such advertisements helped to spread colonial ideas and anchor them in everyday Swiss life.

The fascination with the "exotic" was further evident from the so-called Völkerschauen—also known at the time as "human zoos"—at which "foreign" people, i.e. people from the colonised regions of the world, were exhibited in zoological gardens, theatres, and municipal parks as well as at national exhibitions and circuses. The 1896 national exhibition in Geneva was one such venue: opposite the "Village suisse", which showed an idealised rural Switzerland, the organisers constructed a "Village noir", a "human zoo" with around 227 people from what is now Senegal. These people were defamed as "primitive" and "uncivilised indigenous people", which made it easy for visitors to disassociate themselves from them. Between 1835 and 1964, more than 500 such "troupes" were presented to the Swiss population. The productions were adapted to meet the expectations of the general public, which meant creating and reproducing stereotypical images of the "Other". Those on display included not only professional fairground people but also prisoners of war and kidnap victims who had been illegally transported to Europe. These people were forced to live in precarious conditions, without suitable clothing or a balanced diet; there were regular outbreaks of diseases among them and many died in Switzerland. Meanwhile, the human zoos were lucrative spectacles for the organisers and a popular form of

→ fig. p. 90

entertainment; and they were also used for "racial theory" research. Stereotypical images of the colonies and colonised people were widely disseminated through reports and photos. A good example are the photographs of the Swiss aviation pioneer Walter Mittelholzer (1894–1937), who travelled to the African continent several times between 1927 and 1934 and successfully published books. In his photographs, he portrays people from a perspective that today is considered racist, stereotyping and exoticising. This colonial view of the world manifested itself in numerous reportages about the colonial territories, for example in the newspaper the *Schweizer Illustrierte Zeitung*, as well as in school materials and children's literature. In the popular Globi cartoon books, for example, non-Europeans were always portrayed as childlike, stupid, and helpless people who had to be rescued or enlightened by Globi. From the 1970s onwards, the Globi stories came under growing criticism for depicting foreigners in a derogatory and stereotypical way that created new prejudices or reinforced old ones.

→ fig. pp. 92–95

→ fig. p. 91

Traces of colonialism today

Colonialism and the associated world view have left their mark on the present. Some colonial references are clearly visible, but often go unnoticed by the general public; it is only in recent years that they have been increasingly flagged and discussed again, as, for example, in the case of monuments, street and mountain names, and murals. Other links to colonialism are less visible because they have been forgotten, ignored, or overlaid by new narratives and classifications. Racist stereotypes, in particular, have become deeply rooted in thought patterns, figures of speech, and customs. They are passed on through stories, books, and films and remain powerful to this day.

Just how differently the colonial legacy can be treated in Switzerland is evident from two places named after the zoologist and glaciologist Louis Agassiz (1807–1873): the Agassizhorn in the Bernese and Valais Alps and Agassiz Square in Neuchâtel. Agassiz was not only a natural scientist but also an internationally influential racial theorist and a pioneer of systematic racial segregation. In 2010 and, again, in 2020, the three municipalities of Grindelwald, Guttannen, and Fieschertal rejected a petition by the "Demounting Louis Agassiz" committee to rename the Agassizhorn. In Neuchâtel, on the other hand, the "Espace Louis-Agassiz" square was renamed "Espace Tilo-Frey" in 2019 in honour of the politician Tilo Frey (1923–2008), who was among the first eleven women to be elected to the National Council in 1971, and the first Black woman to sit in federal parliament. It is still the only public square in Switzerland named after a Black person. Since 2023, this pioneering female politician has also been commemorated

→ fig. p. 234
→ fig. p. 235

through *Tilo*, an artwork by the Basel-based Studio Renée Levi that comprises 246 shimmering green ceramic tiles on the tympanum of the Federal Palace.

Bibliography

Brändle, Rea: *Wildfremd, hautnah: Zürcher Völkerschauen und ihre Schauplätze 1835–1964*, Zurich: Rotpunktverlag, 2013.

Dejung, Christof: "Jenseits der Exzentrik: Aussereuropäische Geschichte in der Schweiz", in *Schweizerische Zeitschrift für Geschichte*, 64/2, 2014, pp. 195–200.

Fässler, Hans: *Reise in Schwarz-Weiss: Schweizer Ortstermine in Sachen Sklaverei*, Zurich: Rotpunktverlag, 2005.

Krauer, Philipp: "Zwischen Geld, Gewalt und Rassismus: Neue Perspektiven auf die koloniale Schweizer Söldnermigration nach Südostasien, 1848–1914" in *Schweizerische Zeitschrift für Geschichte*, 71/2, 2021, pp. 229–50.

Purtschert, Patricia, Barbara Lüthi and Francesca Falk (eds.): *Postkoloniale Schweiz: Formen und Folgen eines Kolonialismus ohne Kolonie*, Bielefeld: transcript, 2012.

Purtschert, Patricia: *Kolonialität und Geschlecht im 20. Jahrhundert: Eine Geschichte der weissen Schweiz*, Bielefeld: transcript, 2019.

Zangger, Andreas: *Koloniale Schweiz: Ein Stück Globalgeschichte zwischen Europa und Südostasien (1860–1930)*, Bielefeld: transcript, 2011.

"Village Noir"

The second Swiss Regional Expo, held in Geneva in 1896, presented a "human zoo", with the "Village Noir" forming the main attraction at the amusement park. On display was a troupe of people comprising about 227 people of various ages who hailed from fifteen different West African ethnic groups and were supposed to represent an "African" village.

National exhibition: *Amusement park ("Village Noir")*, 1896, photographer: A. Chevalley, Bibliothèque de Genève, bge 47p expo 896 44 13.

Racism in children's books

"Globi" was created in 1932 by the Swiss cartoonist Robert Lips as an advertising figure for the Globus department store. The Globi stories came in for criticism during the 1970s for depicting non-European cultures in disparaging, stereotypical ways that had the effect of creating or fostering prejudice.

Globi bei fremden Völkern, colouring book, Robert Lips, Globi Verlag, Zurich, 1952, Swiss National Museum.

This photo shows how the photograph of a young Abyssinian woman is staged. The circumstances under which the image was taken are unknown. Walter Mittelholzer's perspective on foreign cultures is influenced by racism and sexism, and one may ask whether he wanted to create a connection between "nakedness" and "savagery" as a counterpoint to the idea of the "moral" woman of middle-class European society.

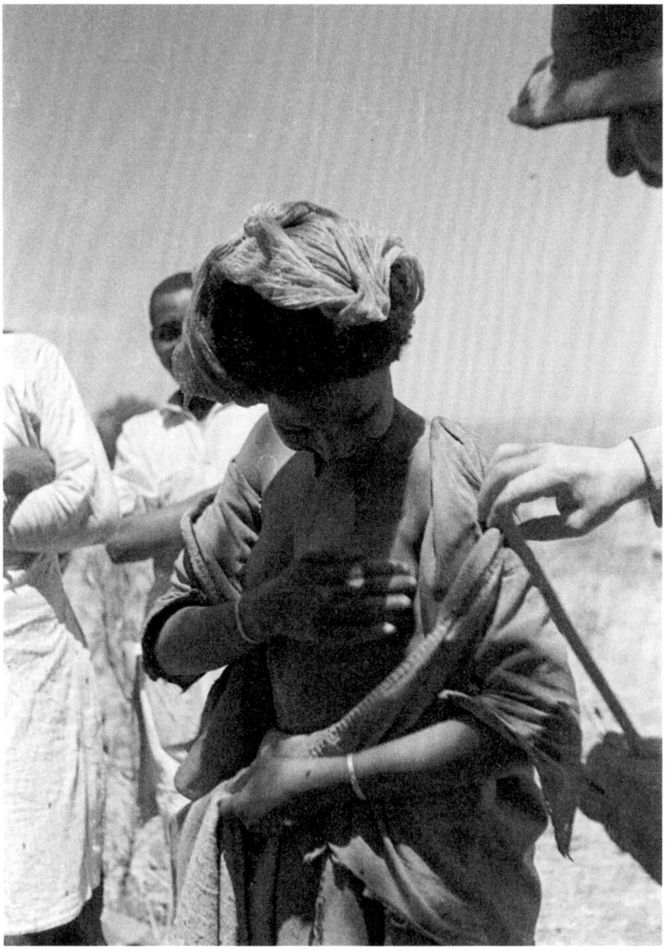

Colonial gaze

Between 1927 and 1934, the aviation pioneer Walter Mittelholzer (1894–1937) undertook several flights to the African continent. In his photographs, he portrayed people from a perspective that today can be described as racist, sexist and exoticising.

Abyssinian woman, photographer unknown, Ethiopia, 1934, ETH-Bibliothek Zurich, Bildarchiv/Stiftung Luftbild Schweiz/LBS_MH02-22-1084.

Group photo

Walter Mittelholzer assembled the servants at a camp in present-day Tanzania for a group photo. The *white* Europeans are seated; the Black men either stand or crouch down—an arrangement that clearly indicates the prevailing hierarchy.

Group photo of the camp's inhabitants, Walter Mittelholzer, Tanzania, 1930, ETH-Bibliothek Zürich, Bildarchiv/Stiftung Luftbild Schweiz/LBS_MH02-07-0316.

Photo session with Haile Selassie I

The purpose of Mittelholzer's flight to Abyssinia was to deliver three Swissair planes to the emperor of Ethiopia, who ruled from 1930 to 1974 and successfully fought Italy's attempt at colonization. Mittelholzer enjoyed privileged access to the monarch; here he staged him in all his royal power and authority.

Kaiser Haile Selassie I, Walter Mittelholzer, Addis Ababa, 1934, reproduction, ETH-Bibliothek Zürich, Bildarchiv, LBS_MH02-22-0396.

Making-of

A cameraman on the flight to Abyssinia took this photograph of a local boy. Making-of images such as this were not reproduced in Mittelholzer's books: as highly staged compositions, their camera angle or the choice of background and props demeaned the subject and implied the subject was somehow different.

Abyssinian boy being photographed, Walter Mittelholzer, Ethiopia, 1934, reproduction, ETH-Bibliothek Zürich, Bildarchiv, LBS_MH02-22-0311.

Fabrics, ships,
and slavery

Switzerland
at the Black Atlantic

Jovita dos Santos Pinto

An estimated twelve million people were abducted from the African continent between the sixteenth and nineteenth centuries, more than half of them in the eighteenth century alone. For every enslaved person who arrived in the Americas, as many as five perished while still in Africa. Some died in the process of being hunted down, others while being marched to the coast or imprisoned in makeshift huts, and still others while chained in the ship's hold off the coast or during the Atlantic crossing.

This all took place in the context of what was known as triangular trade. Europeans would load their ships with goods in European harbours and then sail to Africa where they exchanged them for human beings purchased from Creole, African, and Arab traders. After crossing the Atlantic they would sell these people into slavery and then reload their ships with goods produced with slave labour. These goods were in turn sold upon their return to Europe.

Slavery and transatlantic trade were closely linked with the development of capitalism and European imperialism. They had a destructive impact on Indigenous ways of life on both the African and American continents, resulting in the annihilation not only of people, cultures, and languages, but also—as a result of raw materials extraction and the cultivation of plantations—of animals, plants, and entire ecosystems. Yet it was almost exclusively the cities of the Global North that profited from the value created by these processes. Slavery is part of the *Maafa* (Swahili for "the great misfortune")—the historical, and continuing, systematic violence against black people.[1] It has contributed in key ways to the modern understanding of what it means to be black and to the globalisation and normalisation of racist and anti-black violence. It continues today in the exploitative relationships between the Global North and the Global South.

Triangular trade was closely connected with other trade and enslavement routes that crisscrossed the African continent, the Mediterranean, the Indian Ocean, and the Pacific and led from the coast into the Asian and European hinterland. Africans were not the only people to be enslaved. Europeans engaged in the practice of enslavement elsewhere, too, justifying it with the alleged inferiority of those whom they regarded as Other. This essay will, however, focus on the transatlantic slave trade, the specific form of enslavement whereby human beings were commodified—i.e. reduced to the status of tradeable goods—and on the history of persistent violence against black people.

1 The word "Black" is often capitalised in texts that critique racism. This expresses the fact that it refers to a racist social construction rather than a (skin) colour. Using Black as a political self-designation allows us to visualise specific forms of violence and resistance to them. However, there is also a less well-known practice of lower-casing the term because capitalisation is associated with a liberal understanding of the subject, which in turn is based on dehumanisation, dispossession, and over-exploitation. Especially with regard to the afterlife of slavery, it is not necessarily a matter of being recognised within this order, but of using this non-status as a starting point from which the world can be rewritten. The lower-case b fits this purpose perfectly.

Swiss participation

The territory of Switzerland was already integrated in the global economy in the seventeenth century. Especially from the eighteenth century onwards, Swiss were directly or indirectly involved in the trade in enslaved people, and products based on slave labour changed consumer habits in Swiss cities and rural communities.

A remarkable number of Protestant Swiss families became involved in slavery as traders, investors, plantation-owners, or settlers. Their extensive family networks stretched over the entire European continent, enabling them to play a key role in global trade and to accumulate a large volume of capital.

Chintz—printed cotton fabrics—played a prominent role in the trade in enslaved people. At that time, they were produced mainly in the Netherlands, Germany, and Switzerland. In the eighteenth century, chintz fabrics were the most important commodity to be traded for human beings on the West African coast, ahead of metals, weapons, gunpowder, and alcohol. The close involvement of Swiss companies in this triangular trade was evident in their presence in major harbours, where Swiss were active as manufacturers, traders, and investors, in some cases in all three roles simultaneously—the Neuchâtel-based family business Pourtalès and the Basel firm Burckhardt & Cie. being prime examples.

→ fig. p. 116

→ Andreas Zangger p. 123

→ fig. p. 115

→ fig. p. 141

Trade in enslaved people required major capital investment and promised high returns, but it was also associated with considerable risks and could result in heavy losses and even bankruptcy. Apart from the commodities to be traded, the ship itself, the crew's wages, food, insurance, etc. had to be paid for. For Swiss financiers both private and state—like the Zinskommission Leu, for example—enslavement expeditions were promising investments, which they treated like any other branch of business. Trade in enslaved people was an early form of modern speculative finance.

A considerable number of Swiss were involved in the plantation economy, administering and owning plantations in the Caribbean, in Brazil, and in the United States. There they also founded large "colonies" whose origin is still reflected today in place names like Nova Friburgo or New Bern. They served in colonial administrations as stewards or as traders in goods produced by the labour of enslaved people, whom they often also owned. Swiss mercenaries likewise helped to keep the plantation economy going. They put down uprisings, hunted down fugitive slaves, and waged war on their hidden settlements in the interior. In the late eighteenth century, people from socially disadvantaged segments of the population began emigrating from Switzerland to the colonies, hoping to escape poverty and precarious circumstances. Many of them made fortunes, which they subsequently used to build grand residences back home and to invest in the Swiss infrastructure.

Human life as a commodity

A number of fragments of stories of enslaved and liberated people, such as Pedro (?–1792) and Vendredi (?–1793) in Neuchâtel, François Midas (?–1797) and Pauline (?–1826) and her son Samuel Buisson (1790–1832) in Yverdon, and Ernesto Braganza (?–c. 1885) in Zurich, have survived. They reveal that Switzerland, like most other European countries, was not a slave-owning society, but one society in which enslaved people lived. While their fate differed from those of enslaved people in plantation economies, they highlight a racist exclusion that still resonates today.

→ Philipp Krauer p. 143

→ fig. p. 146

In the transatlantic slavery regime, enslaved people were degraded to the status of capital and commodities that could be owned and traded, thus destroying their social existence. This is reflected in historiographical sources, in reports of terror and atrocities, and in banal figures and dimensions: 40 cm of space for every enslaved person on a ship, 11 so-called Trade Ounces as the standard price for a human being on the West African coast. Lists of people transported as freight, the insured value of the load, and calculations of the risk posed by rebellions, of the value of healthy, sick, or dead slaves, and the anticipated profit—all these things treat sex, age, state of health, disability, and mutilation not as social but as economic factors. These mathematical and economic values provide information not only about the costs, profits, and losses of Swiss traders in their trade with enslaved people; they are also an expression of the violent social relationships created by the regime of slavery. The geographer Katherine McKittrick calls this "the mathematics of the unliving", stating that these figures not only testify to social violence in the past but also serve to perpetuate epistemic violence in the present by abstracting the humanity of these people.

Resistance

Where does resistance against slavery begin? Dancing, singing, and religious gatherings, for example, were tolerated by slave-owners in the Americas and in some cases even promoted as a means of increasing productivity. Through slow working, feigned illness, visiting one another at night, or storytelling enslaved people sought to collectively alleviate their suffering and established a form of community where none was supposed to exist. There were also more direct forms of resistance, such as poisoning livestock, arson, strikes, or uprisings. Escape into the hinterland or joining forces in gangs were social forms of resistance against slavery that have to date received little attention. Fugitives and formerly enslaved people formed resistance communities known as the Marronage, the Cimarrones, or the Quilombos, while the "Underground Railroad" was one of several organised escape routes from the states of the American South to Canada which managed to survive for decades. Black people thus developed forms of collective living and infrastructure while on the run, joining forces with free, poor, Indigenous, and *white* people and anyone else who showed solidarity with them. They also launched attacks and raids on plantations and hatched plans for the (unaccomplished) liberation of other enslaved people. The Quilombo Helvécia community in Brazil, where the descendants of enslaved people still live in the German-Swiss settler colony Leopoldina today, testifies not only to Swiss exploitation but also to the resistance to it.

→ fig. p. 120/121

Swiss mercenaries in the service of imperial nations helped to put down such collective solidarity movements and rebellions, including—from the early eighteenth century—in Haiti, where attempts to combat the independence movement ultimately proved unsuccessful. The revolution staged there by black people culminated in 1804 in the liberation of all enslaved people on Haiti. Its goal was a radical redistribution of resources and it provided inspiration for liberation struggles worldwide, sending a shock through the global racial order, which until then had seemed unshakeable. Both Switzerland and other European countries generally failed to recognise the significance of this revolution. Revolutionaries, abolitionists, and slavery apologists alike sought to play it down. In contrast to *white-led* revolutions, that on Haiti was interpreted as proof that black people were intrinsically violent "savages". In return for international recognition as an independent state, Haiti was forced to pay compensation to France equivalent to 32.5 trillion Swiss francs in today's terms. Former Swiss plantation owners also claimed annuities for the loss of their estates. These debts, together with an international embargo, transformed the young state within a short space of time from the world's largest sugar exporter into what is today still one of its poorest countries.

Abolition

Haiti was no exception. All European countries that abolished slavery before 1850 negotiated financial compensation and annuities for the former owners of enslaved people, but not for the enslaved people themselves. What is more, in most cases the plantations were returned to their former owners. Poverty, transitional arrangements, a ban on vagrancy, and other new laws often forced formerly enslaved people to continue working on the plantations either bound by contracts or extralegally. While a few of them managed to rise socially, the official abolition of slavery brought no improvement to the living conditions of the majority. Instead of ending enslavement practices, it often meant their continuation and extension under different social and legal auspices.

In Switzerland, as in the rest of continental Europe, abolition between the mid-eighteenth and mid-nineteenth centuries tended to be addressed sporadically and as an elite discourse. Participants in this discourse included Swiss with ties to international Protestant banking and trading networks, such as the Coppet-Gruppe in which Germaine de Staël (1766–1817) was the central figure, and not least Swiss publishers, who issued abolitionist texts and literature for dissemination in France.

Not until the second half of the nineteenth century, after the prohibition of transatlantic trade in enslaved people, did an independent abolitionist movement evolve in Switzerland. Popular reports, bestsellers such as *Uncle Tom's Cabin,* and photos like "The Scourged Back, 1863" circulated widely, making the atrocities of slavery visible. At the same time, they helped to popularise racist ideas about black people as passive victims who were reliant on the help of *whites*, ideas that are still used to mobilise humanitarian donations today. The terrible beauty of such images made the violence inscribed into the bodies of black people common knowledge—but also made it seem normal. Yet Europeans learned little about enslaved people's own ideas about freedom or indeed about Gordon himself, whose back was displayed to the entire world.

In Switzerland abolition was discussed in missionary magazines and liberal-conservative, anti-slavery societies. Large sums of money were collected to buy the freedom of enslaved people and to support them once freed. This new, pan-European movement was shaped by Christian morals and, following the prohibition of slavery in the United States in 1865, focused on the slave trade on the African continent. However, Switzerland's own historical involvement in this trade tended to be downplayed and the discourse restricted to an anti-Muslim one about Arab traders, who were portrayed as backward and uncivilised. At the height of the European "scramble for Africa", abolition was closely linked with European colonial policy.

The wide range of agendas behind Swiss abolition is demonstrated by the example of Wilhelm Joos (1821–1900), a member of the National Council. In 1863 and 1864 he called three times for the citizenship of Swiss who had bought or sold enslaved people in Brazil to be revoked, thus indirectly providing the Swiss government with an opportunity to take up an anti-slavery position. Joos was in fact less concerned about enslaved people than about Swiss sharecroppers. He thought the abolition of slavery ought to lead to a greater appreciation of their labour and thus to an improvement in their living conditions. These were people who had hoped to escape poverty in Switzerland by emigrating. Having incurred debts in order to finance their passage, they were now tied to major landowners, where their living conditions deteriorated further. Joos's first two motions were rejected by the Federal Council; on the second occasion the reason given was that this was not in Switzerland's political interests. Joos's proposal for a third motion was rejected by the parliament from the outset.

Until well into the twentieth century, abolitionism in Switzerland often merely served to legitimise new capitalist forms of exploitation and to justify colonisation and missionary activity in Africa. And even today the abolition of slavery has still not been fully accomplished. The call for abolition, which came to the world's attention more widely with the Black Lives Matter protests in 2020, is an appeal to end anti-black violence once and for all and finally honour the promise of freedom.

Barros, Izabel, and André Nicacio Lima: "Geschichte Dekolonisieren – Ein kritischer Beitrag zu einer globalen Schweizer Geschichte" in Anisha Imhalsy, Rohit Jain, Manuel Krebs, Tarek Naguib and Shirana Shahbazi (eds.): *Handbuch Neue Schweiz, INES – Institut Neue Schweiz,* Zurich/Berlin: Diaphanes, 2021, pp. 135–158.

Brahm, Felix, and Eve Rosenhaft (eds.): *Slavery Hinterland: Transatlantic Slavery and Continental Europe, 1680–1850*, Woodbridge: The Boydell Press, 2016.

dos Santos Pinto, Jovita: "Besitzen, s/exotisieren, vergessen—Schwarze Geschichte in der Schweiz um 1800" in *RosaRot. Zeitschrift für feministische Anliegen und Geschlechterfragen*, 56, 2019, pp. 39–43.

Fässler, Hans: *Reise in Schwarz-Weiss: Schweizer Ortstermine in Sachen Sklaverei*, Zurich: Rotpunktverlag, 2020 [2005].

Hartman, Saidiya: *Lose Your Mother: A Journey Along the Atlantic Slave Route*, New York: Farrar, Straus & Giroux, 2008.

McKittrick, Katherine: "Mathematics Black Life" in *The Black Scholar*, 44/2, 2014, pp. 16–28.

Malinckrodt, Rebekka von, Josef Köstelbauer and Sarah Lentz (eds.): *Beyond Exceptionalism: Traces of Slavery and the Slave Trade in Early Modern Germany, 1650–1850*, Oldenburg: De Gruyter, 2021.

Robinson, Cedric J.: *Black Marxism: The Making of the Black Radical Tradition*, Chapel Hill: The University of North Carolina Press, 2020 [1983].

Thomas, David, Bouda Etemad and Janick Marina Schaufelbuehl: *Schwarze Geschäfte: Die Beteiligung von Schweizern an Sklaverei und Sklavenhandel im 18. und 19. Jahrhundert*, Zurich: Limmat, 2005.

Schär, Bernhard: "Slavery, Exoticism and Swiss Exceptionalism around 1800" in Noémie Étienne, Claire Brizon Claire, Chonja Lee and Étienne Wismer (eds.): *Exotic Switzerland? Looking Outward in the Age of Enlightenment*, Zurich: Diaphanes, 2020, pp. 63–78.

Stettler, Niklaus: *Baumwolle, Sklaven und Kredite: Die Basler Welthandelsfirma Christoph Burckhardt & Cie. in revolutionärer Zeit (1789–1815)*, Basel: Christoph Merian, 2004.

Mathias Pfund

Great in the concrete, 2022, Bronze.

Swiss National Museum.

Toppling monuments

In 2021 the Geneva-based artist Mathias Pfund placed his upended and reduced-scale copy of the statue of David de Pury alongside the original that was raised in Neuchâtel in 1855. David De Pury (1709–1786) was a banker and diamond trader with interests in the "triangular trade" and who therefore had a hand in the transatlantic slave trade.

Remis gratuitement aux donateurs

BULLETIN

DES

Amis des Esclaves

Organe de la Société Suisse de secours aux Esclaves africains.

Mars 1897. N° 13.

Un asile d'esclaves inattendu.

Le Comité des Missions de Bâle nous communique le rapport suivant dont M. Ramseyer nous avait annoncé la prochaine arrivée et qui intéressera sans doute nos lecteurs; nous n'y avons fait que quelques coupures sans importance.

Quatrième année.

The anti-slavery movement in Switzerland

After 1860, Switzerland was among the countries in which major, anti-slaver movements were established—most of them with their roots in religious circles. The focus now shifted to combating the trade in enslaved people in Africa organised by Arab dealers.

Bulletin des Amis des Esclaves. Organe de la Société Suisse de secours aux Esclaves africains, William Kündig, Geneva, March 1897, no. 13, Bibliothèque de Genève, BGE E 1866.

Captured

These U-shaped shackles were used on children, women, and men, mostly on their feet. Either one person would be shackled by both ankles or two enslaved people would be chained together to limit their mobility and thus prevent escape or rebellion.

Shackles for restraining hands and feet, West Africa, before 1900, Collection of the Basel Mission, deposited 1981, gifted 2015, Museum der Kulturen Basel, III 26264, photo: Omar Lemke, 2023.

Neither the clothing of the seller (Spanish/Portuguese dress of the early sixteenth century) nor that of the trader (a Turkish/Arabic coat) allows us to identify them unambiguously. The manufacturer, the Kilchberg-Schooren factory, provides no clues either: two of the owners had links to abolitionist circles, while two others had connections with people involved in the trade with enslaved people.

Slave trade

This group of figures depicts the sale of an enslaved person. The clothing of the figures leaves plenty of scope for interpretation, and it is unclear whether the object is meant to support or oppose slavery.

Slave trade, porcelain figure group, Manufaktur Kilchberg-Schooren, Kilchberg, c. 1775, Swiss National Museum.

The way human beings were itemised alongside other trade goods shows that enslaved people were sold like commodities. Alongside the transatlantic European trade, there was also a corresponding trade within Africa and Arabia. Researchers estimate that the latter alone was responsible for the enslavement of over 17 million people from Africa and 1.25 million people from Europe.

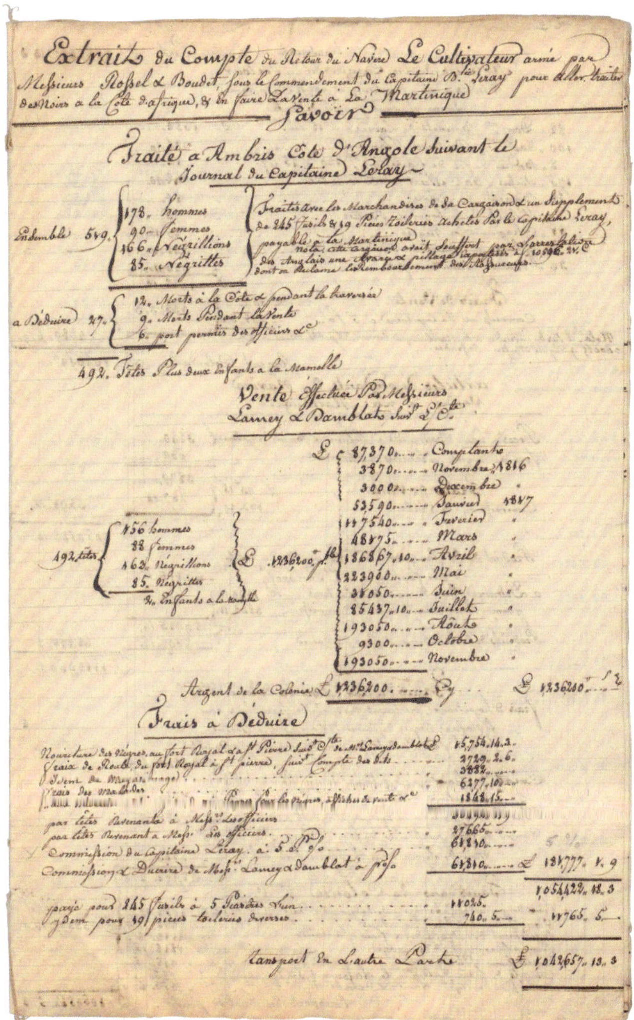

Manufacturer, trader, investor

Christoph Burckhardt & Cie. was a Basel firm that produced chintz fabrics and traded in colonial goods. The Burckhardt family participated in twenty-one voyages that abducted 7,350 enslaved people to various destinations.

Excerpt from an invoice for the slave ship, Christoph Burckhardt & Cie., Basel, 1815–1817, Swiss Economic Archives, Basel, SWA HS 420 N 1-10.

Fabric for the trade in enslaved people

This fragment may be the only surviving example of a chintz cotton print fabric produced by a Swiss manufacturer especially for the purpose of being exchanged for enslaved people.

Le lion et la chèvre, indiennes, Manufacture Petitpierre & Cie., Nantes, late 18th century, woodblock print on cotton fabric, Swiss National Museum.

Historical depictions and sources employ terms that are no longer used today. The “N word”, which is derogatory for Black people, is closely linked to the history of colonialism, slavery, and so-called “racial theories”. The curators of the exhibition have retained the term in historical sources and depictions. However, they employ a dash in our own descriptions to avoid reproducing racist language.

Martial art

Calinda is a martial art as well as a style of music and dance practised by enslaved Africans in the Caribbean. François Dumoulin (1753–1834) travelled from Vevey to Grenada in 1773 to create landscapes and plans for the British governor. As a painter, he was interested in the lives of enslaved people on the island.

Calinda, danse des N— en Amérique, François A. L. Dumoulin, 1783, Musée historique de Vevey.

Denise Bertschi

Helvécia, Brazil, embroidery on cotton fabric, St. Gallen, 2017.

Musée d'art et d'histoire de Neuchâtel, photo: Timo Ullmann.

Helvécia

Archival documents show that Swiss plantation owners in Brazil owned enslaved people. The St. Gallen technique of eyelet embroidery testifies to gaps in the documentation. The fabric panels contain the names of the enslaved people and stamps of the Swiss consulate.

Dom Smaz

Dona Cocota, published in the book *Helvécia*, photography, Brazil, 2015.

Swiss National Museum.

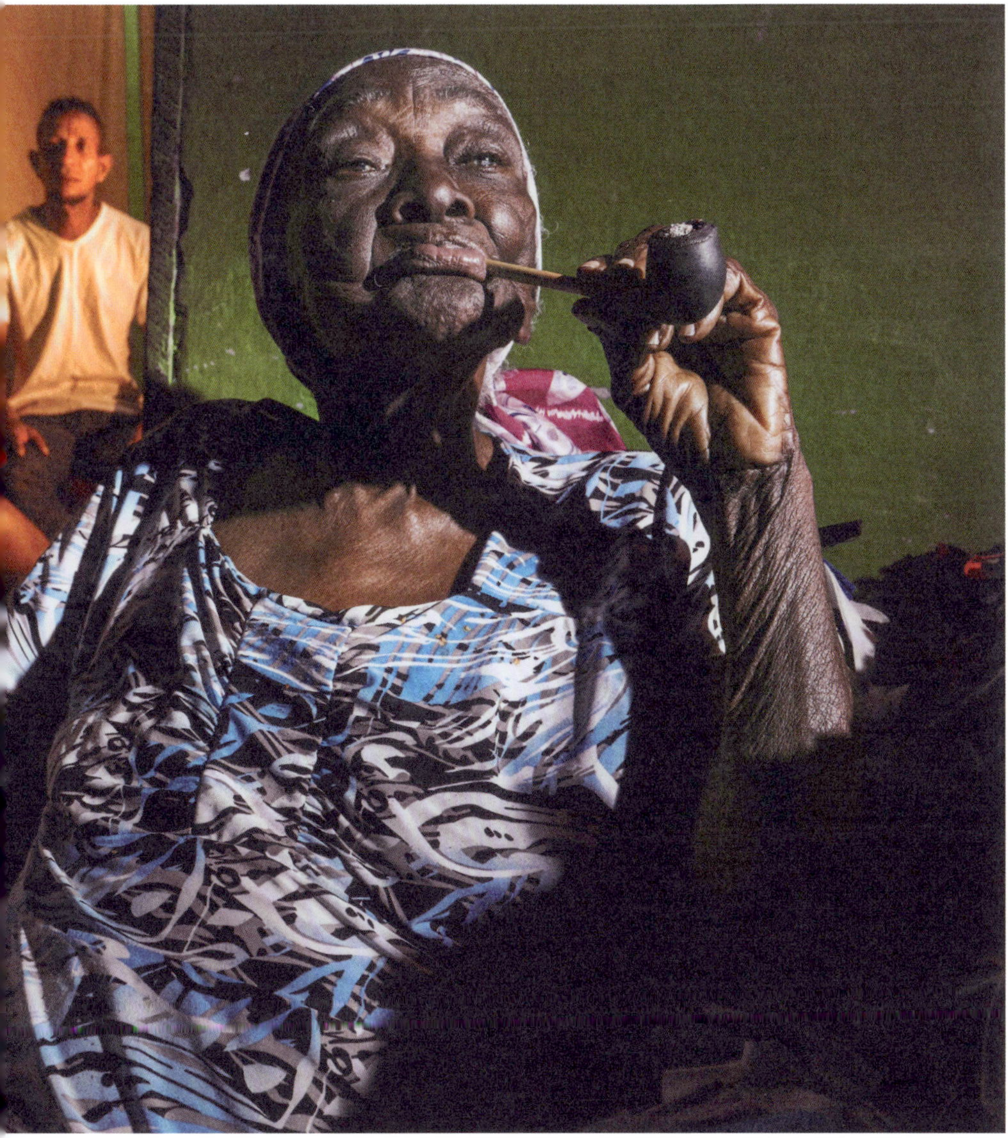

A quilombo with a Swiss past

Less than a century after the founding of the Leopoldina colony, the traces of the Swiss plantain owners have almost disappeared. The enslaved people remained. Their descendants tell the story of Helvécia, an Afro-Brazilian village, whose Swiss name reminds us of its past.

Jumping on the bandwagon of colonial exploitation

Swiss wholesale trade in the colonial era

Andreas Zangger

Colonial trade in the early modern era was fraught with violence. Barter, robbery, and piracy were all intimately connected. The Spanish mercilessly plundered American gold and silver. In Asia, first the Portuguese and then later the Dutch used violence as a means of imposing trade monopolies. And the "triangular trade" across the Atlantic involved the abduction of over twelve million people, mainly from Africa to America, as well as extreme exploitation on the plantations producing commodities such as cotton, indigo, coffee, and sugar, which in turn acted as a driving force for European industrialisation. According to the theory of mercantilism, colonial trade promised to supply the great European nations with an abundance of precious metals. This meant they were engaged in ongoing trade wars with each other, often leading to armed conflict

As a weak commonwealth of states, the Swiss confederation was unable to participate in this rivalry. Merchants in Switzerland consequently pursued two strategies in order to muscle in on global trade. Caught in the slipstream of Switzerland's political irrelevance, they tried to create personal advantages and established international networks. Their operations were based in European seaports, from where the ships departed to Africa or America. They became skilled in exploiting identities to their advantage and would claim to be from Geneva or St. Gallen when it suited them—but then pretend to be French if that better served their purpose. In the early modern era, this was an option open only to a few wealthy patrician families. The somewhat less affluent families only became involved in the international trade business from the nineteenth century onward. This model of operating in fluid networks favoured by the economic elite, preferably without state interference, is a recurrent feature of Swiss history trade.

Investment in the slave trade
and the trade with chintz

While Swiss merchants initially became involved in transatlantic trade via capital investments, their indirect participation in textile production played a more significant role. Apart from weapons, what the trading companies primarily needed was fabrics known as chintz, which could ← fig. p. 116 be exchanged for enslaved people. At first these fabrics came predominantly from India, but as demand grew in Europe and in transatlantic trade, Europeans began producing replicas. This would have been impossible without the existence of a well-established cottage industry at home—and this too is an indirect consequence of colonialism. The glut of gold in Spain pushed up prices for yarn and fabrics, which in turn made the—albeit limited—exploitation of homeworkers worthwhile. Merchants with links to European seaports had these fabrics printed to suit individual markets and then exported them. Those with international connections were able to amass great wealth. The homeworkers, however, became increasingly dependent on merchants who were operating on an international scale.

The production of chintz fabrics along with industrialisation in general drove the trade with colonial products. For chintz, one required cotton as well as various dyes and fixing agents such as indigo (a blue dye), cochineal (a red dye predominantly from Mexico), colouring woods from Brazil, and the binding agent gum arabic (from Senegal). Industrialisation, in turn, created a strong demand for coffee and sugar among the working population.

Textile exports to distant markets

The early textile industry was able to build on the networks and experiences of the long-distance traders of the ancien regime. As Thomas David and Bouda Etema have established, industrialisation in Switzerland was characterised by its exceptionally high reliance on far-flung markets in its early stages. This was due to tariff barriers raised by neighbouring countries as well as the ability to exploit a technological advantage over foreign markets. The watch industry had blazed the trail, as it were, by establishing trade routes that would also facilitate the textile business: southern Italy became a major export market from the 1810s onwards, with Latin America following from the 1820s, the Ottoman world from the 1830s, and South-East Asia from the 1850s. Several factories in Switzerland even started producing textiles for the Japanese market in 1865.

Merchants had to be present in these locations to sell the fabrics. At least in the main markets, manufacturers were happy to cooperate with Swiss people, who had undergone training in the industry. This facilitated the spread of the Swiss textile trade (in a similar manner to watch-making and cheese exports) across all continents with the help of network-like structures. Many merchants established links with existing, predominantly German, trading companies, hoping to become independent later on, given the opportunity.

In the mid-nineteenth century, three short-lived trading companies emerged in Switzerland that attempted to systematically promote the sale of Swiss industry products through representative offices overseas: Union horlogère (1858–1866) for the watch-making industry, St. Galler Handelsgesellschaft (1862–1866) for textiles, and Schweizerische Exportgesellschaft (1857–1870) for both textiles and machines. The latter had close links to the Schweizerische Kreditanstalt. The ambitious project involved branches in Thessaloniki, Tabriz, Aleppo, Baghdad, Valparaiso, Natal (Brazil), Calcutta (today Kolkata), Bombay (today Mumbai), and

Shanghai. The focus was on markets where there was no threat of competition from local (mechanised) industries. But the individual branches soon ran into difficulties because the large structure turned out to be too inflexible, and, at the same time, it proved almost impossible to keep things under control from such a large distance.

The historian Herbert Lüthy once observed that "a merchant who is based there and truly at home there, who purchases significant quantities of the country's products, who has close personal ties to the host country and has become familiar with the conditions there over many decades," was more effective than agents abroad. Indeed, the survival of the trading companies was dependent on their not only selling textiles and other goods from Europe but also buying local products and shipping them to Europe. This was how large profits were made. But such a business model also bore significant risks because prices tended to fluctuate considerably. Therefore, Swiss merchants often cooperated with Hanseatic counterparts, who had more experience in the commodity trade. There are numerous examples of this kind of collaboration in Brazil, India, South-East Asia, and Africa.

The career of Wilhelm Heinrich Diethelm from Thurgau was typical in this respect. After a commercial apprenticeship in the textile industry and sojourns in Paris and London, his supervisor found him a job with an overseas trading partner, where he was responsible for selling textiles.

In Diethelm's case, this was a Dutch trading company in Singapore, at the time one of the largest markets. After more than a decade he was able to take over the company. In order to communicate with Indian and Chinese merchants he had to learn Malay. Establishing trust with intermediaries and maintaining regular contact with them were decisive factors in his success, because they only paid for the textiles after the goods had been sold. Retaining good links to the producers in Europe was similarly important. They had to be constantly provided with information concerning levels of demand and pattern trends. Even back then, fashion was an extremely fast-paced business.

Some Swiss trading companies shifted their focus to the commodity, with Volkart & Co. being the most prominent example. Having originally sold Swiss textiles in India, the company soon started trading Indian raw cotton instead. The company was reacting to—and at the same time encouraging—the process of de-industrialisation in India, because now the cotton was exported to Europe rather than being refined locally. In the eighteenth century, India had been the biggest cotton producer in the world, exporting fabrics to Japan, South-East Asia, Europe, Africa, and Mexico. A century later, production had largely disappeared due to cheap imports from England and Europe. Volkart steadily expanded its network of branches and factories in India, later in other countries, too, so that in the twentieth century the company became a global leader in the cotton trade as well as in the coffee business.

The Basler Handelsgesellschaft (which later became the Union Trading Company, or UTC) has an extraordinary history to tell. With its roots in the Basel Mission, its function was to assist the organisation's operations and also provide a boost to its finances. It supplied the missionary posts in India and Ghana with the European goods they needed and traded wholesale cocoa, palm oil, and cotton in the other direction. Some of the profits flowed back into the missionary work. The initiator of this system was Ulrich Zellweger, member of a well-known family of merchants from Trogen, who was familiar with the practices of colonial trade thanks to his trading company in Cuba. The Basler Handelsgesellschaft was involved in the introduction of cocoa culture in Ghana and retained a prominent role in the cocoa business up until the First World War.

Swiss silk-trading companies in Japan also succeeded in dominating the export market until 1900, with a quarter of the volume accounted for by one firm, Siber & Hegner. Japan may not have been a colony, but it only truly opened up to Western trade after the Americans put military pressure on the country in the mid-1850s. Switzerland was then able to conclude a favourable trade agreement with Japan, following in the wake of the colonial powers. Merchants from Zurich and Basel swiftly established themselves there, not least on the basis that they supplied the silk industry in both those cities with raw silk. However, Japan caught up quickly and began processing and exporting local silk independently.

→ fig. p. 133

A graphic of the Volkart company and its branches illustrates the kind of business networks that companies constructed. The links criss-crossing the globe made up part of a business's capital. As Swiss, rather than being confined to the boundaries of colonial empires, they sought out niches in the network and connected various world regions with each other. This is why Lea Haller calls the major Swiss merchants the "engineers of globalisation". Yet they always enjoyed the protection of the colonial powers and refused to be drawn into any activities beyond the military and legal influence of imperial powers. Moreover, in most places they were able to capitalise on the groundwork laid by minor trading communities that had long been internationally active, such as the Chinese in South-East Asia, Gujaratis in East Africa, Armenians in the Ottoman Empire, Parsis in India, Lebanese in West Africa, etc. Not only were these individuals needed as trading partners, in some cases they were also employed as staff in charge of liaising with local traders.

By the 1930s, the number of Swiss-owned or partially Swiss-owned trading companies had fallen sharply. Some were sold when the owner returned to Switzerland. Others lost their Swiss ties, particularly when the company passed into

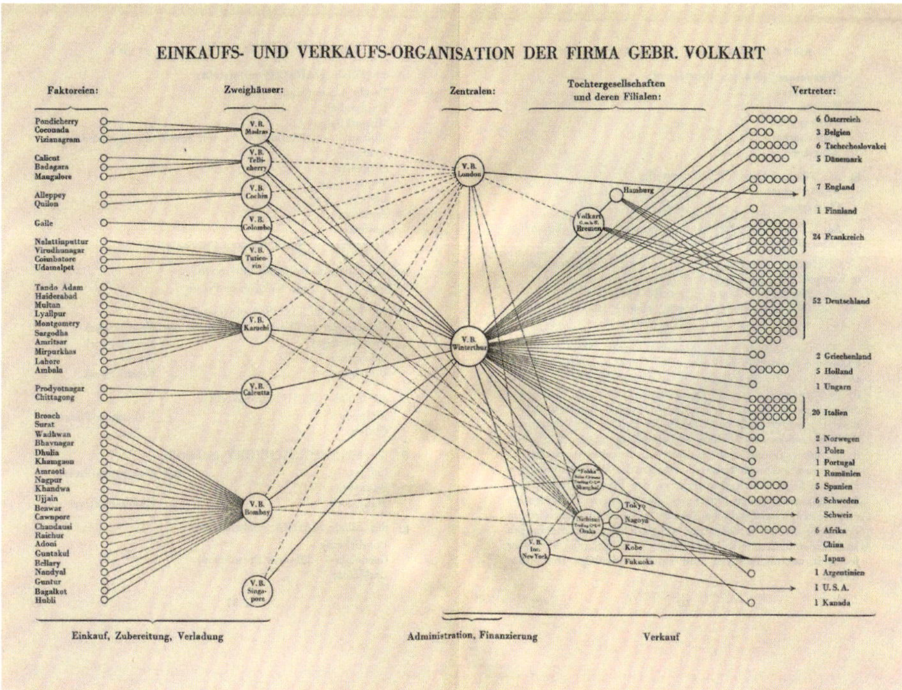

Trade network

The graphic shows the financial and trade streams in the global network of the Volkart colonial goods company. Raw materials were bought by purchasing agents, while subsidiary companies were responsible for selling them on to the industrial sector. All the threads came together in Winterthur.

The organisation of buying and selling at Volkart Bros., map, 1925, Winterthur City Archive, Volkart Bros. company archive, Dep 42/951.

the hands of a new generation that had closer links to the new location than with Switzerland. Companies relying on German investors ran into serious difficulties in the First World War.

Some wholesale traders, however, were able to consolidate their position and continued to grow despite the Great Depression. While trading companies in the nineteenth century were still primarily engaged in the import/export business, the focus shifted to transit trade in the twentieth century, i.e. Switzerland was no longer the ultimate destination of the goods being traded, but merely the country where the sales transactions were conducted. The transit trading companies developed the tools and infrastructure that would enable this, in conjunction with the major banks and many smaller financial service providers. Swiss politicians facilitated the growth of the sector by introducing favourable legal frameworks at home. Swiss wholesale and transit trade thus became a prominent aspect of the economy without ever attracting too much public attention, nor did the sector itself—which attached great value to secrecy—go looking for publicity.

Against this backdrop, various large international trading companies have set up their headquarters in Switzerland since the 1980s, and now dominate the list of the country's largest corporations, handling around 20 to 25 per cent of global trade in the most important commodities. Little has changed with respect to trading conditions since the colonial era. The countries of origin still only derive minimal benefit from the profits of commodity chains, yet they bear the greatest burden in terms of environmental harm.

David, Thomas, and Bouda Etemad: "L'expansion économique de la Suisse en outre-mer (XIXe-XXe siècles): un état de la question" in *Schweizerische Zeitschrift für Geschichte*, 46/2, 1996, pp. 226–231.

Dejung, Christof: "Unbekannte Intermediäre: Schweizerische Handelsfirmen im 19. und 20. Jahrhundert" in *traverse, Zeitschrift für Geschichte*, 17/1, 2010, pp. 139–155.

Dejung, Christof: *Die Fäden des globalen Marktes: Eine Sozial- und Kulturgeschichte des Welthandels am Beispiel der Handelsfirma Gebrüder Volkart 1851–1999*, Cologne: Böhlau, 2013.

Franc, Andrea: *Wie die Schweiz zur Schokolade kam: Der Kakaohandel der Basler Handelsgesellschaft mit der Kolonie Goldküste (1893–1960)*, Basel: Schwabe, 2008.

Gilomen, Hans-Jörg, Margrit Müller and Béatrice Veyrassat (eds.): *Globalisierung: Die Schweiz in der Weltwirtschaft, 18.–20. Jahrhundert*, vol. 19, *Schweizerische Gesellschaft für Wirtschafts- und Sozialgeschichte*, Zurich: Chronos, 2004.

Guex, Sébastien: "Development of Swiss trading companies in the twentieth century" in Geoffrey Jones (ed.), *The multinational traders*, London: Routledge, 1998, pp. 150–172.

Haller, Lea: *Transithandel Geld- und Warenströme im globalen Kapitalismus*, Berlin: Suhrkamp, 2019.

Hauser-Dora, Angela Maria: *Die wirtschaftlichen und handelspolitischen Beziehungen der Schweiz zu überseeischen Gebieten 1873–1913 unter Berücksichtigung der konjunkturellen Entwicklung*, Europäische Hochschulschriften, vol. 320, Bern: Peter Lang, 1986.

Iselin, Isaak, Herbert Lüthy and Walter S. Schiess: *Der schweizerische Grosshandel in Geschichte und Gegenwart*, Basel: Selbstverlag der Delegation des Handels, 1943.

Peyer, Hans Conrad: *Von Handel und Bank im Alten Zürich*, Zurich: Berichthaus, 1968.

Siegenthaler, Hansjörg: "Die Bedeutung des Aussenhandels für die Ausbildung einer schweizerischen Wachstumsgesellschaft im 18. und 19. Jahrhundert" in Bernard Nicolai (ed.): *Gesellschaft und Gesellschaften: Festschrift zum 65. Geburtstag von Professor Dr. Ulrich Im Hof*, Bern: Wyss, 1982, pp. 325–340.

Veyrassat, Béatrice: "1945–1990: Bilan des recherches sur l'histoire du négoce international de la Suisse" in *Schweizerische Zeitschrift für Geschichte*, 41/3, 1991, pp. 274–286.

Veyrassat, Béatrice: *Histoire de la Suisse et des Suisses dans la marche du monde*, Neuchâtel: Livreo-Alphil, 2018.

Welter, Karl: *Die Exportgesellschaften und die assoziative Exportförderung in der Schweiz im 19. Jahrhundert*, Bern: Stämpfli, 1915.

In the 19th century, advertising for consumer products became widespread, and a specific visual vocabulary emerged for “exotic” products such as chocolate. Here, a hierarchy is drawn between a domestic worker and a black servant. In the context of the patriarchal, racist society of the time, the young boy is doubly belittled: because of his black skin color, he finds himself in the position of a servant and, what's more, subordinate to the housewife or female employee.

Suchard chocolate

Suchard was one of the world’s largest chocolate manufacturers in the late nineteenth century. The dominant success of Swiss chocolate was possible only thanks to cocoa from Ghana and the links between the chocolate industry and the growing dairy business.

Chocolat Ph. Suchard, Imprimerie F. Champenois Paris, Neuenburg, 1898, Zurich University of the Arts / Design Museum / Poster collection, 61-0494.

Merchant ship

This three-master was commissioned in 1859 by J. C. Kuhn, a Swiss cotton merchant and consul in Texas, for use as a merchant ship. A year later, it sailed to Liverpool with its first cargo of cotton picked by enslaved men and women.

Samuel Walters, *View of Johann Conrad Kuhn's ship*, Liverpool, 1859, oil on canvas, Swiss National Museum.

Gunny sack

Christoph Burckhardt & Cie., a trading company based initially in Basel and later in Nantes, engaged in global trade in cotton and chintz along with other colonial goods. The company was also involved in the trade in enslaved people and was responsible for approximately twenty voyages on which about 7,350 people were abducted to the Americas.

Linen sack from Christoph Burckhardt & Cie., c. 1800,
Basel Historical Museum, photo: Natascha Jansen.

Because the Basler Missionshandelsgesellschaft was a member of the cartel of European trading companies, it was able to push producers' prices down, thereby obstructing competing African companies on the market. The cocoa trade was nationalised in 1947, putting an end to the cartel. For a long time, the cocoa trade was the backbone of Ghana's economy.

Drying cocoa in Accra

Founded in 1859, the Basler Missionshandelsgesellschaft (BMG) was an offshoot of the Basel Mission. Until 1879, the company traded in cocoa and grew its own cocoa plants. From 1921 onwards, the BMG becomes the Union Trading Company; one of Switzerland's largest trading companies.

Accra, drying cocoa, c. 1904/1905, archive of the Basel Mission, Q-11-30.003.5ff.

Indian workers

Volkart Bros. was a cotton trading company. Raw cotton was processed in the hinterland using cotton gins and steam presses prior to being exported. Volkart established several presses and began operating its first cotton gin in the early twentieth century.

Ginning plant in Nagpur, 1914, Stadtarchiv Winterthur, Firmenarchiv Gebr. Volkart, Dep 42/1840.16.

Krüsi Manager House

Karl Krüsi (1855–1925) worked for Swiss plantation owners in the Sultanate of Deli on Sumatra. He bought his own plantation in 1881 and named it after his Javanese-American wife, Mary Ganno (1852–?). He sold the plantation in 1893 after his exploitation of his workforce and nature had made him a wealthy man. In Zurich, he built Villa Sumatra.

Manager House in Deli, Maryland Estate, Karl Krüsi, Deli, 1885, Swiss National Museum.

On money and violence

The global dimensions of Swiss mercenarism

Philipp Krauer

In many respects, the history of European colonialism is a history of violence. European trading companies and states gained access to markets and resources by means of force in Asia, Australia, Africa, and North, Central, and South America. Several million colonial soldiers participated in the subjugation of peoples overseas. They guarded plantations on which enslaved people worked, they sought to maintain an inner order based on racial hierarchies, and they defended colonised territories against outside rivals. However, hardly any of the colonial powers could meet their need for military personnel by recruiting at home. To fill the gaps, they could either recruit troops in the colonies themselves, or they could hire the services of European mercenaries. Tens of thousands of Swiss served in colonial armies. By recruiting Swiss mercenaries, colonial powers profited from existing structures in the European mercenary markets that date back to the Middle Ages.

Swiss soldiers had enjoyed a good reputation among European royal and princely houses at least since the Burgundian Wars (1474–77), and, consequently, these dynasties repeatedly recruited entire regiments of Swiss mercenaries. The treaties on the deployment of troops generally stipulated that they may only be deployed in Europe. As European powers began to expand overseas, however, a global mercenary market began to develop alongside the intra-European market. Initially, large numbers of Swiss were recruited by the West

This painting is believed to be the only surviving portrait of enslaved people working in a Swiss household in the eighteenth century. It reveals that there was an upper class in Switzerland that owned enslaved people. Virtually nothing is known about most enslaved people in Switzerland, since the few extant sources provide hardly any information about the lives and experiences of these persons.

Pedro and Vendredi

Charles Daniel de Meuron (1783–1806) returned to Switzerland in 1786. Two years later, he had two of the twelve enslaved people that were in his possession shipped from Cape Town to Switzerland. Pedro (?–1792) and Vendredi (?–1793) came from Mozambique and India, respectively. They succumbed to a respiratory infection in the winter of 1792/93.

Josef Reinhard, *Image of Charles-Daniel de Meuron and two men*, 1789, oil on canvas, Musée militaire et des toiles peintes, Colombier.

and East India Companies in England and the Netherlands, usually on an individual basis, and these numbers continued to rise during the eighteenth century. The French crown also made use of Swiss mercenaries to defend their overseas territories. An examination of the biography of Charles-Daniel de Meuron illustrates just how permeable the boundaries between the continental and global mercenary markets truly were.

Charles-Daniel de Meuron (1738–1806)

De Meuron was born in St Sulpice in the Canton of Neuchâtel in 1738 and began a commercial apprenticeship at the age of thirteen. In 1755 he left civilian life behind and joined the French Hallwyl marine infantry regiment, a unit founded by the Swiss Franz Adam Karrer (1666–1740) with outposts in Louisiana (USA), Saint Domingue (Haiti), and Martinique. During the Seven Years War (1756–63), de Meuron was sent from the French garrison town of Rochefort to the Caribbean colonies to protect sugar plantations worked by enslaved people from English attempts to seize them. Two years later and after a number of naval engagements, he was granted six-months' leave and returned to Switzerland to recuperate from the wounds he had sustained in battle. He then returned to Rochefort, where he married the wealthy Anne-Marie Filhon de Morveaux (1733–1809).

← fig. p. 146

When the Hallwyl Regiment was disbanded in 1763, de Meuron decided to continue his career as a trader in colonial goods. Two years later, however, he returned to the military and enlisted as an officer in the French king's Swiss Guards unit. His continuing fascination with the colonies led him to the idea of establishing a Swiss settler regiment for French Guyana at his own expense. His suggestion was initially ignored, and after sixteen years of service he left the Swiss Guard. That same year he was recruited by the Dutch East India Company (Vereenigde Oostindische Compagnie, VOC) to raise a colonial regiment, and in May 1782 the unit sailed for the Cape of Good Hope. Unlike his soldiers, de Meuron led a luxurious life while stationed there, and a staff of at least twelve enslaved persons catered to his creature comforts.[1] He returned to Europe in 1786 to negotiate with the VOC about additional expenses he had incurred. He transferred command of the regiment to his younger brother Pierre-Frédéric (1746–1813), and shortly after the latter's arrival, the VOC ordered the regiment to Ceylon (Sri Lanka), where it was tasked with protecting the company's profitable cinnamon plantations.

The regiment's later fate was determined by global political events. When French troops invaded the Netherlands in 1795, the VOC was met with financial difficulties and found itself unable to pay its mercenaries. This turn of events was exploited by the British, who lured the Meuron

Regiment away from its former employer and used it to conquer Ceylon. In order to organise the transfer to British service, Charles-Daniel de Meuron bequeathed his anthropological and natural history collection, which included a number of objects acquired during his time at the Cape of Good Hope, to the city of Neuchâtel before travelling to South Asia. His brother remained in command and was promoted to brigadier general, and from 1797 to 1798 he even served as the military governor of Ceylon. Charles-Daniel initially remained in South Asia, from where he sent additional collection items back to Neuchâtel. In 1797 he finally returned to Switzerland via London and Berlin. His regiment remained in British service and was deployed around the world. It fought in the Fourth Anglo-Mysore War against Tipu Sultan's troops and took part in the subsequent plundering of the southern Indian city of Sriringapatna. In 1808 it was transferred to Malta and in 1813 to Canada, where it was disbanded in 1816.

Transformation of the mercenary market in the nineteenth century

The Meuron Regiment existed during a transitional period in which the mercenary market was fundamentally transformed. In the wake of the 1814/15 Congress of Vienna there was an upsurge in intra-European mercenary services, with a number of Swiss regiments fighting in the service of Spain, France, the Netherlands, and the Kingdom of the Two Sicilies, albeit usually only for relatively short periods of time. In 1823 the Spanish court discharged its Swiss troops. The Netherlands terminated its mercenary contracts with the Swiss cantons in 1829, France followed suit in 1830, and in 1859 the Swiss regiments stationed in Naples were dismissed.

Whereas intra-European mercenary regiments were finally viewed as a relic of the past and were replaced with national armies, the colonial mercenary market began to grow in importance, for unlike the wars in Europe, colonial wars were rarely fought with conscript soldiers. Instead, the colonial powers relied on a mix of volunteer citizens, Indigenous soldiers, and mercenaries. For example, between 1815 and 1962, up to 40,000 Swiss served in the French Foreign Legion and 7,600 in the Dutch colonial army. As a member of the latter, the Grisons-born mercenary Hans Christoffel achieved dubious fame.

Hans Christoffel (1865–1962)

Unlike de Meuron, Christoffel came from a humble background: his parents were farmers in Rothenbrunnen. Beginning in 1882 he attended the cantonal school in Chur, which he left without graduating. Travelling to the Netherlands in 1886, he joined the colonial army there. While we have no information about what motivated Christoffel to take this step, we know from other Swiss mercenaries that the desire to emigrate often arose out of a mix of financial difficulties, a lack of prospects, and a lust for adventure. Ultimately the colonial armies, in addition to lucrative pay, regular income, and a lifelong pension, also offered men the opportunity to travel the world for free. A week after his arrival at the military base in Harderwijk, Christoffel was sent to the Dutch East Indies (Indonesia).

His first six years of service on Java and Ambon were relatively peaceful. However, his situation changed when he was transferred to Aceh on the north-western tip of Sumatra in 1892. Since 1873, the Netherlands had been trying to subjugate the previously independent Sultanate. Due to intense resistance, what was originally planned as a quick "military expedition" soon developed into a war lasting over forty years that cost the lives of around 75,000 Aceh inhabitants as well as, on the Dutch side, 25,000 colonial soldiers, relatives of auxiliary troops, and forced labourers.

Christoffel now found himself fighting at the front. In 1902 he was transferred to the Korps *Maréchaussée te voet*, a special unit comprised of Indigenous soldiers led by European officers that had been fighting in "anti-guerilla" operations since 1895. The unit achieved notoriety when, from February to June 1904, it marched through Sumatra's mountainous backcountry, armed with modern repeating rifles, and left a trail of destruction in its wake. It is estimated that the troops killed anywhere from five to twelve per cent of the Indigenous Gajo and around twenty per cent of the Alas peoples. The extent of the violence caused outrage in Europe. A Dutch member of parliament noted: "It is as if a band of bloodhounds had been turned loose against the *Inlanders*."[2] Christoffel's participation in the massacres had no negative impact on his career. Quite the contrary, in fact, for in 1905 he was assigned to lead his own brigade, the infamous "Tiger Column". In the following years he was stationed at a number of locations where he defended the Dutch claim to sovereignty against the resistance of the Indigenous population: on Borneo (Kalimantan) in 1905, on Celebes (Sulawesi) in 1906, in Aceh in 1907, on Flores from August 1907 to March 1908, and in Aceh again in 1908. Christoffel considered any means justified: torture, executions, and kidnappings of family members were among the most often employed measures.

The brutality of Christoffel and his soldiers is illustrated by a campaign conducted on Flores. In only seven weeks, his troops murdered over 700 people on the island. As the anthropologist Edgar Keller and his colleague Yoseph Agato Sareng showed some 100 years later, some of the victims' descendants still recall the acts of extreme violence. For example, Thomas Mite, a resident of the village of Masu in the So'a region, told the

→ fig. p. 153

Memories of a colonial massacre

In 2023, the Zurich ethnologist Edgar Keller and his colleague Yoseph Agato Sareng produced a short film with interviews with residents of Flores whose parents and grandparents witnessed the massacres of 1907 ordered by Hans Christoffel. In the film, Thomas Mite and Franziskus Rema Lawa talk about the mass murder of the population of their village.

Thomas Mite and Franziskus Rema Lawa, set photo, Masu on Flores in Indonesia, 2023, Swiss National Museum.

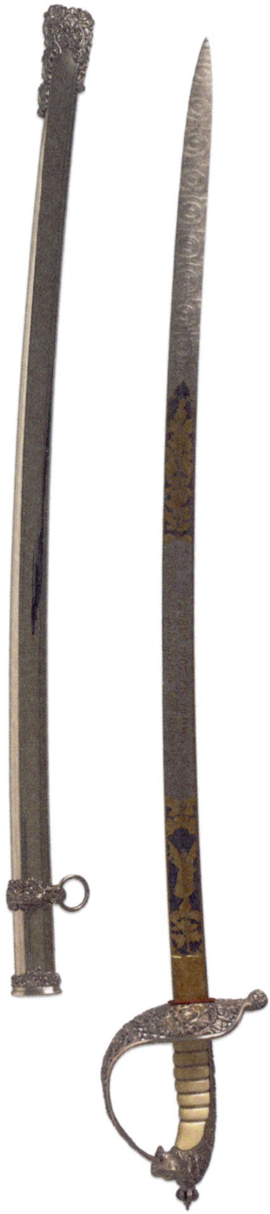

Awarded instead of convicted

After his campaigns in Aceh, Hans Christoffel (1865–1962) travelled on to Flores where his dreaded "Tiger Column" committed further massacres. For his brutal actions, which also caused outrage among Europeans, Queen Wilhelmina of the Netherlands awarded him with an honorary sabre.

Engraved honorary sabre, 1908, Collection Museum Bronbeek, Arnhem.

anthropologists how his father had only narrowly escaped death at the age of ten. According to his account, Dutch troops approached the village around noon. The approximately 100 village inhabitants present at the time fled to nearby caves, where heated discussions broke out. Around half of them, including Mite's father, felt the caves offered insufficient protection, so they moved on. The remainder stayed in place—with fatal consequences. The colonial soldiers discovered their hiding place and opened fire. From what the villagers tell us, only three of them survived the massacre by hiding under the corpses of their own relatives.[3]

The atrocities on Flores came under severe criticism from many sides. However, Christoffel's superiors continued to back him, and, instead of facing trial, he was awarded an honorary sabre for his efforts on the island. When he was discharged in 1910, Christoffel, who had acquired Dutch citizenship four years previously, was one of the most highly decorated officers in the colonial army. His rise in society was also reflected in his private life. While on leave in Europe in 1909, he married Adolphina Anna Maria Martha van Rijswijk (1881–1960), the daughter of a former mayor of Antwerp. After he was discharged from military service in 1910, the couple initially remained in the Dutch East Indies, where Christoffel worked as a concession hunter. Twenty years later they moved to Antwerp. Christoffel donated countless objects that

← fig. p. 154

he had purchased, stolen, or plundered during his time in South-East Asia to the local museum.

Ramifications of global entanglement

The biographies of de Meuron and Christoffel represent only two among countless life histories that illustrate the complex history of colonial mercenarism. An additional aspect of this history are the contacts between Swiss mercenaries and Indigenous women. Far away from the social control of their home environments, many mercenaries lived together with Indigenous concubines who functioned as cultural intermediaries, ran the household, nursed sick soldiers, and cared for their joint children.

Furthermore, colonial mercenary networks were also important for individuals who themselves never left Switzerland, since the veterans' pensions usually also benefited their wives and children. Even though these payments were often small, they could make a significant difference. Moreover, Swiss colonial engagement had a cultural impact at all levels of society, from the privileged upper class to farmers and proletarians. The stereotypical world views acquired within the racist context of the colonies, which suggested the superiority of *white* Europeans, were communicated by returning mercenaries to their relatives and friends. In the case of de Meuron, this racism was manifested in concrete terms: From the Cape of Good Hope he had two enslaved men named Pedro (?–1792) and Vendredi (?–1793) sent to Switzerland in 1788. They died of respiratory infections in Switzerland in the winter of 1792/93.

← Jovita dos Santos Pinto p. 97

1 The names and sale prices of the enslaved persons are listed in the object inventory that de Meuron sold upon his return to Europe in 1786. Archives de l'État de Neuchâtel, fonds RÉGIMENT MEURON, Dossier No. 14. VI, Traduction du Rolle de ventes faites dans la maison de Monsieur le Comte & Colonel de Meuron, au Cap de bonne Espérance les 21 & 22 Mars 1786.

2 "Het is of men op de inlanders een bende bloedhonden heeft losgelaten." Victor de Stuers, cited in Veer, Paul van 't, *De Atjeh-oorlog* (Amsterdam 1969), p. 277.

3 I would like to thank Edgar Keller and Yoseph Agato Sareng for providing me with the notes they made during their visits in 2007 and 2008. Zangger also provides an account of this story. See Andreas Zangger and Hans Christoffel: "Ein Bündner Jagdhund in Indonesien" in *Die Wochenzeitung*, 15 August 2019. A confidential report compiled by the Royal Netherlands East Indies Army lists thirty-nine victims. Ministry of War report, 1 September 1908, p. 14, in Nationaal Archief, Den Haag, Ministerie van Koloniën: Geheim Archief [periode 1901–1940], nummer toegang 2.10.36.51, inventarisnummer 104.

Bijl, Paul: *Emerging Memory: Photographs of Colonial Atrocity in Dutch Cultural Remembrance*, Amsterdam: Amsterdam University Press, 2015.

Durinx, Willy, Paul Catteeuw, and Roselyne Francken: "De collectie Hans Christoffel in het MAS Antwerpen" in *Volkskunde Journal*, 3 (2019), pp. 473f.

Groen, Petra et al.: *Krijgsgeweld en kolonie: Opkomst en ondergang van Nederland als koloniale mogendheid, 1816–2010* (Amsterdam: Boom, 2021).

Henry, Philippe and Philipp Krauer: "Fremde Dienste" in *Historisches Lexikon der Schweiz* (HLS), https://hls-dhs-dss.ch/de/articles/008608/2023-10-31/ (accessed 31 Oct. 2023).

Kaehr, Roland: *Le mûrier et l'épée: le cabinet de Charles Daniel de Meuron et l'origine du Musée d'ethnographie à Neuchâtel*, Neuchâtel: Musée d'ethnographie, 2000.

Krauer, Philipp: *Swiss Mercenaries in the Dutch East Indies: A Transimperial History of Military Labour, 1848–1914*, Leiden: Leiden University Press, 2024.

Lee, Chonja: "Von Zucker, Indienne und versklavten Menschen: Materielle Spuren des transatlantischen Handels in der Alten Eidgenossenschaft" in Schweizerisches Nationalmuseum (ed.), *Barock. Zeitalter der Kontraste*, Zurich: Christoph Merian, 2022, pp. 70–75.

Lesueur, Boris: *Les troupes coloniales d'Ancien Régime: Fidelitate per Mare et Terras, Kronos N° 82*, n.p.: SPM, 2015.

Meuron, Guy: *Le Régiment Meuron, 1781–1816*, Lausanne: éditions d'en bas, 1982.

Rial, Sébastien (ed.): *De Nimègue à Java: Les soldats suisses au service de la Hollande; XVIIe-XXe siècles*, Morges: Château de Morges et ses musées, 2014, pp. 237–23.

Swiss missionary
societies and colonialism

Religious, cultural,
and political entanglements

Claudia Buess

The activities of European missionary societies all over the world have an ambiguous history. While there is evidence of respectful contact with local populations, we also find records of Eurocentric arrogance and aspirations to dominance. The relationship between missionary activity and colonialism was a complex one that manifested itself in a variety of ways. Switzerland too was involved in colonial and missionary expansion from the beginning, with Swiss Jesuits working as missionaries in the territories conquered by the kings of Spain and Portugal as early as the sixteenth century.

Protestant missionaries, by contrast, did not take up their activities until the eighteenth century and stepped up their work in the nineteenth century. In most cases, these were lay missionaries working for private, ecumenical organisations. The rise of such missionaries followed the development of an enlightened bourgeoisie in Europe and an aspiration to spread civilisation that was construed as a mandate to disseminate the Christian faith. One of the first Protestant missionary societies in Europe was the Basel Mission (BM), which was founded in 1815—during the heyday of colonialism—by wealthy Pietist citizens from the economic, political, and religious elites of Basel. The missionaries of the BM, at first exclusively and later predominantly male, came from the artisanal and peasant classes of southern Germany and Switzerland and underwent six years of training before being sent to the Gold Coast (1828, modern

Ghana), southern India (1834), or China (1846). French-speaking Switzerland became involved as well: the late nineteenth century marked the beginning of missionary activities by the Protestant free churches of the cantons of Vaud, Geneva, and Neuchâtel. Their joint missionary society, Mission Suisse Romande, continued the activities which the Free Church of Vaud had begun in 1875 in southern Africa (South Africa and Mozambique).

Swiss missions as part of a religio-political internationalism

Like their Catholic counterparts, the Swiss Protestant missionary societies adhered to a "religious internationalism" based on the guiding principle of spreading the Kingdom of God throughout the world. They were embedded in transnational religious networks in which Protestant missions from Europe supplied personnel to one another, maintained a variety of contacts, and met at international missionary conferences. While the European states were launching the "Scramble for Africa" at the "Berlin Congo Conference" in 1884/85, German missionary societies, including the BM, were engaged in intense discussions concerning their stance on colonialism at the Continental Mission Conference in Bremen. Should the missions place themselves at the service of a nation state, or should they preserve their independent, international character? Ultimately, both paths were taken in the colonised missionary regions, since the ideal of the supranational, apolitical missionary movement soon came up against the pragmatic limitations of the reinvigorated nationalism of the European countries in the nineteenth century—especially in those regions where colonial powers were competing for land and natural resources. Thus, missionary societies in the colonies were operating within a complex web of relationships involving a variety of actors: colonial administrations, Indigenous populations, settlers, other missionary societies, and local and global economic structures. While all these aspects facilitated cooperation, they also gave rise to unholy alliances and, in certain cases, to conflicts of interest. Working with transnational political networks was not only unavoidable but also useful if the societies wanted to perform their task of converting the local populations with as little hindrance as possible.

Cooperation, conflict, and unholy alliances

Based in neutral Switzerland, the BM too had extensive contacts on the international religious and political scene. It skilfully promoted its interests in the colonised missionary areas through its direct connections to the parliaments and administrative offices of the colonial powers. In the case of Cameroon, for example, a conflict with the German colonial authorities arose in 1898. The BM opposed the colonial administration's expropriation of land owned by the Indigenous population, since—as Horst Gründer has shown—this practice also placed their own missionary activities and landholdings in jeopardy. Petitions made to the Protestant Missions' office at the Imperial Colonial Office in Berlin and to Reichstag deputies resulted, inter alia, in the recall of the colonial governor. The dealings of missionaries with colonial authorities were always dominated by their interest in being able to pursue their work of evangelising the local population as efficiently as possible.

The nineteenth-century Gold Coast, modern Ghana, provides a vivid example of the complexity of the entanglements and situational alliances among which the BM operated in regions under colonial rule. As Peter Haenger's excellent dissertation has shown, the missionaries met with resistance from some of the local Asante rulers who rejected Christian missions as an alien cultural influence. Seeking to expand its missionary activities into the heart of the Asante empire, following in the wake of British colonial forces, the BM supported the formal establishment of a crown colony in Asante territory in the interior. However, since the British Empire hesitated to do so for various reasons, the BM went as far as sending the missionary Elias Schrenk (1831–1913) to lobby the British parliament in 1865. His efforts, however, were initially unsuccessful, and it was not until 1874 that the British, after several violent campaigns, subjugated the central Asante government in Kumasi, and the BM gained access to the former Asante provinces. According to Peter Haenger, the missionaries were "aware [...] of the unholy alliance of Bible and cannon—without developing feelings of guilt about it."

This unholy alliance even extended to the BM providing logistical support and supplying soldiers from their Christian parishes for the British colonial troops (as it did for the German colonial troops in Cameroon during the First World War). The British government sent a note of thanks to the Swiss federal president for the services of the BM during the subjugation of the Asante in 1874. Around the turn of the twentieth century, the BM deployed the missionary Otto Lädrach (1875–1949) as a military chaplain in Ghana at the request of the British colonial army and also supplied around 350 Indigenous Christians for another British campaign against the Asante.

The Mission Suisse Romande, for its part, was involved in complex alliances with the colonial authorities of South Africa and Mozambique. In 1907, in order to be able to continue its work despite a shortage of funding, it accepted the segregated schools introduced by the British colonial Transvaal government in return for subsidies for its Lemana Teacher and Catechist Seminary. In 1898, the missionary Georges Liengme (1859–1936), who had been forced to leave Mozambique in 1896 after being involved in a rebellion against the Portuguese colonial government, established separate hospitals for Black and *white* people at the behest of Paul Kruger (1825–1902), the president of the South African Republic—because this was the government's condition for funding missionary health services for the Black population. Here, then, the missionaries supported or profited from racist colonial administrative structures, which were permanently entrenched by the South African government in the apartheid system in 1948.

From paternalism to cultural imperialism?

To be able to spread the Gospel efficiently, Swiss missionaries were active in a number of areas: education, health services, and skilled trades. The BM established factories and a trading company that would later become the Missionshandelsgesellschaft. This approach represented the beginnings of "Christian development aid". In India, it opened up opportunities for social advancement to members of low castes. Christian ethics also formed the basis for the BM's rejection of any and all forms of enslavement. In 1861 (fourteen years before the British colonial authorities), its leaders banned the possession of enslaved people by Indigenous Christians in its communities on the Gold Coast (Ghana) and established a "Slave

Emancipation Committee" that enforced the liberation of enslaved people—despite the reservations of individual Christian missionaries. Slave-owning Christians had to free enslaved people within two years or be expelled from their community.

The purpose of converting the local population to Christianity, educating them, and giving them work was to enable them to participate in progress and attain wealth as defined by European standards. The primary goal of the missions—both the Mission Suisse Romande and the BM—was to convert the locals and turn them into educated Christians. The precepts of the mission societies held that conversion to the Christian faith, which was regarded as a higher level of development and civilisation, was only possible in conjunction with a life of hard work and abstinence. According to historian Karolin Wetjen, it was almost impossible to keep apart the task of conversion and the mission to civilise since both conveyed specifically Eurocentric Christian values.

Although both the BM and the missionaries from French-speaking Switzerland cared about the Indigenous populations, produced Bible translations, and compiled dictionaries that represented outstanding contributions towards documenting local cultures and languages in image and writing, they also acted as staunch representatives of the western European Protestant faith and culture which they regarded as superior.

Once again it becomes evident that the work of the missionaries was double-edged: their publications, mass-distributed to solicit donations and extremely popular, sometimes disseminated paternalistic and even discriminatory or racist depictions of people from non-European cultures. Occasionally, they also contain deprecating descriptions of local belief systems, social structures, and cultural practices that were to be replaced by the Christian faith. Even if such views were widespread at the time, what we see here is a form of cultural imperialism that was also reflected in the second half of the nineteenth century by scientific racism.

According to Patrick Harries, such depictions allowed the Swiss public to consolidate its own identity as members of a progressive Christian nation—at a time when the Federal Republic was still young and Switzerland displayed a multiplicity of cultural, linguistic, and economic differences. Moreover, the publications allowed the Swiss public to participate in the "civilising mission" without becoming involved in its violent and repressive side. As a country without colonies of its own, Switzerland was thus able to profit from colonialism not only culturally and economically but also ideologically—an aspect that Switzerland is only too keen to downplay in its public self-image. The ways in which colonialism, economic interests, and the civilising mission were interwoven were explicitly addressed early on by Henri A.

Junod (1863–1934), the missionary, ethnographer, and botanist from Vaud who wrote the following in 1928 to mark the fiftieth anniversary of Mission Suisse Romande: "Switzerland is not a colonial power. It could have easily denied itself an interest in Africa. It did not take this path. Swiss merchants opened their offices in African cities and thus helped us people of the Occident to benefit from Africa's treasures. Swiss churches heard the call and ministered to the enormous throngs of the N—. They seek to improve and raise the religious, social, and moral condition of the Africans by sending numerous missionaries."

Feigk, Matthäus: "Die transnationalen Netzwerke protestantischer Missionsgesellschaften nach dem Ersten Weltkrieg und das Missionstreffen von Oegstgeest 1920", www.europa.clio-online.de/essay/id/fdae-1707 (accessed 26 July 2023).

Gründer, Horst: *Christliche Mission und deutscher Imperialismus: Eine politische Geschichte ihrer Beziehungen während der deutschen Kolonialzeit (1884–1914) unter besonderer Berücksichtigung Afrikas und Chinas*, Paderborn: Ferdinand Schöningh, 1982.

Haenger, Peter: *Die Basler Mission im Spannungsbereich afrikanischer Integrationsversuche und europäischer Kolonialpolitik, Asante-Mission Abetifi/Kwawu 1869–88*, licentiate dissertation in history, Basel: Universität Basel, 1989.

Harries, Patrick: *Butterflies & Barbarians: Swiss Missionaries & Systems of Knowledge in South-East Africa*, Oxford: Ohio University Press, 2007.

Jeannerat, Caroline, Éric Morier-Genoud, and Didier Péclard: *Embroiled: Swiss Churches, South Africa and Apartheid*, Zurich: Lit, 2011.

Jenkins, Paul: "Die Basler Mission im kolonialen Spannungsfeld Indien: Eine Einladung zu Imperialismus- und Nationalismusforschung im Archiv der Basler Mission" in *Traverse: Zeitschrift für Geschichte*, 5/2, 1998, pp. 41–55.

Junod, Henri A.: *Fünfzig Jahre Schweizer Mission in Südafrika*, Zurich: Wanderer, 1928.

Lädrach, Otto: "Afrikanische Kriegserinnerungen" in *Mitteilungen aus Asante: Kollekteblatt des Berner Hilfsvereins für das Missionswerk in Asante (Afrika)*, 18/80, 1919, pp. 1–12.

Missionary world map

This world map of 1891 shows regions in which Protestant and Catholic missionaries were working. Pictures of "heathens" illustrate the mission's intention: the Christianisation of all peoples on earth.

Missionary world map, Verlag der Missionsbuchhandlung, Basel, 1891, Basel Mission Archive, BMA KARVAR-31.080.

Catherine Mulgrave (Gewe)

Gewe (1827–1891) was abducted from Angola to Jamaica as a child and enslaved. After attaining her freedom, she became a teacher. She married a Ghanaian member of the Basel Mission, and the two opened several schools in Ghana. In 1851, she married her second husband, the German missionary Johannes Zimmermann. She worked as a teacher and took care of her family.

The Zimmermann-Mulgrave family, unknown location, 1873, Basel Mission Archive, QS-30.002.0237.02.

Until 1901, women were not allowed to work as missionaries. Their only chance was an arranged marriage with a missionary. Many women were willing to go abroad to an unknown husband in order to be able to live an independent life at the side of their husband. Not until 1901 did the Basel Mission begin recruiting unmarried women for missionary work.

Diary of a missionary

Maria Müller-Kapff, the wife of missionary Wilhelm Müller (1871–1958) in Kalikut (Kozhikode), India, describes the situation during the First World War when missionaries were interned by the British. Her husband was taken into protective custody.

Diaries about some experiences in India during wartime, 1914–1915, Maria Müller-Kapff, Basel Mission Archives, BM A-80.12.01.4.

Mission romande

In the late nineteenth century, three Free Churches in western Switzerland came together to form the *Mission romande*. One of their mission stations was in Elim in the Transvaal (part of modern South Africa), where they established missionary schools, seminaries for training Tsonga teachers, preachers, and pastors, and a hospital.

Mission romande du Transvaal, postcard, Elim, Chapelle, undated, private property, Patrick Minder, Fribourg.

Travelling to the mission station in a sedan chair

As late as the 1930s, a member of the Capuchin order still travelled to her mission station (presumably in West Africa) in a sedan chair. The image of the *white* woman who allows herself to be carried and the large group of Black men who bring her to the mission station illustrates the hierarchy of the relationship between the missionary and the local population.

Caravan of carriers, collection of travel images from the Mahenge region, c. 1930, Provincial Archive of the Swiss Capuchins, Lucerne, PAL FA II, 45.1.

Statue of a European

An artisan from the Rikatla Mission carved this statue that Henri-Alexandre Junod (1863–1934) presented to the museum in Neuchâtel around 1900. It depicts a European colonial official. This type of object, which is also known from other regions but is still little noticed, is remarkable because it reverses the direction of the gaze. An inhabitant of the colonised area creates a kind of caricature of a European.

Statuette représentant un Européen, collection of Henri-Alexandre Junod, Rikatla, 1911, Musée d'ethnographie de Neuchâtel.

Resistance Art

Purchased by the Swiss missionary Henri-Alexandre Junod in what is now Mozambique, the sculpture shows a leopard killing an Englishman. The sculpture was inspired by a piece in the art collection of Tipu Sultan, showing a tiger devouring an English soldier. "Tipu's Tiger" served as an inspiration for artists worldwide.

Léopard dévorant un Anglais, sculpture, Mouhlati, Lourenço Marques (modern Maputo), c. 1896, wood, Musée d'ethnographie de Neuchâtel, photo: Alain Germond.

Sandeep TK

From the series *Let me add something in my own melody*, 2020.

Courtesy Sandeep TK.

Basel Mission tile

The artist Sandeep TK's photographic works commemorate the Basel Mission, which maintained schools, a brickyard, and a technical institute in Kerala. The picture shows Sandeep TK in front of the Indian brickyard, wearing a *dhoti*, a garment that was regarded as "backward" during the British colonial era.

Researching, collecting, preserving

Swiss explorers in colonial territories

Tomás Bartoletti

The relationship between science, collections, and imperialism that has been at the core of recent debates about the colonial legacies of European museums is encapsulated in the following questions: To what extent are all sciences imperial? Is knowledge production always colonial? These questions can be answered in the affirmative in a swift, but rather simplistic way. Such responses come at the price of losing the nuances surrounding the complexities of scientific enterprises in the last centuries, a period usually defined as the modern age and connected with the expansion of a capitalist global economy backed by European imperial powers. Over the past decades, studies of the social and political conditions of knowledge formation have become mainstream for historians of science and scholars in related fields. Yet the question of the "globality" of sciences has raised new concerns regarding the solely European origins of botany and all scientific disciplines. Knowledge formation has been and is always the result of interactions between women and men of different societies and class status. These interactions, however, are not grounded in neutral and equal conditions but in uneven, asymmetrical relationships. The colonial in sciences is defined, then, by the types of interactions and power structures that shaped how various forms of knowledge were and are constituted. Collections in museums and universities are only the tip of the iceberg of scientific knowledge formation and colonialism over the past centuries.

The coloniality of knowledge refers also to the kind of imaginary about scientific authority and epistemic hierarchies. Both have been the consequence of outdated histories of science that served to establish teleological narratives of modernisation and Western exceptionalism. Inspired by scientific explorations around the world, like those of Charles Darwin and Alexander von Humboldt in the nineteenth century, the histories of "global" science have forged an explanatory description of the quest for knowledge as adventure and action. For those histories, the sciences turned to the global when European travellers discovered the "New World" and far-off lands in Asia, Africa, the Pacific territories, and the Poles, which later became part of the colonialised world. Such narratives are no longer taken for granted. On the contrary, scholars have shown in recent years that the scientists involved depended on the support, labour, and knowledge of Indigenous and non-European people. These new perspectives have dismantled ideas about the "Great (White) Men of Science", ideas that have been popularised in school manuals, through monuments, and through the names given to universities and research institutes.

European scientists collected a massive number of plants, insects, birds, arrows, ceramics, stones, and objects of different kinds from every corner of the world. Collecting was, indeed, a crucial part of the "scientific" conquest to which their journeys were dedicated. Objects served to witness the treasures of the pan-European undertaking of knowing all environments and societies across the globe. The same collections in European museums are today the material evidence of the fact that science was an essential tool of imperialism, exerting violence of different kinds and diffusing racist ideas of European supremacy.

Swiss collections today hold high amounts of animal and plant specimens, human remains, and palaeontological fossils, usually acquired in faraway places and in contexts of colonial domination. These collections demonstrate the deep entanglement of Swiss scientists with European imperial powers, and can certainly be considered part of "colonial science". Yet scientific enterprises also operated in the hidden spaces of empire. For example, when South American states achieved independence in the nineteenth century, science still served to spread ideas of European supremacy and to prospect for profitable natural resources. Scientific collecting based on "race science", which included both human remains and anthropological artefacts, played a key role in justifying not only the social structuring of the new South American states but also the global prominence of European nations in the ordering of a world economy. Like their European peers, Swiss scientists made a considerable contribution to filling the shelves of many museums and university repositories with skulls and ceramics.

Colonial science and nineteenth-century exploration

The period between approximately 1750 and 1950 saw expansive overseas exploration by European empires. Scientific expeditions travelled to distant places and accumulated massive collections. In this context, a paradigmatic case of Swiss science in colonial spaces is the 1838–1842 expedition by the naturalist Johann Jakob von Tschudi. This expedition is representative of the kind of colonial entanglements that have shaped many Swiss collections. It also sheds light on the association between scientific institutions and the emerging Swiss bourgeoisie with its desire for global trade expansion in the first half of the nineteenth century. Moreover, this case reintroduces Swiss actors into the history of early nineteenth-century scientific exploration around the globe, undertakings that are usually associated with the much-studied expansionist aspirations of the British, French, Prussian, and Habsburgian Empires.

Born and raised in the Alpine canton of Glarus, Tschudi moved at a young age to Zurich, where he became a good friend of Alfred Escher in the cantonal school. As well as acquiring an education in Greek, Latin, and Hebrew philology, both men learned natural history from Rudolf Schinz. This professor was known as the populariser of natural history through illustrated publications including manuals of European mammals and the "human races". His book *Naturgeschichte und Abbildungen der Menschen und der verschiedenen Rassen und Stämme* (Natural history and images of people and the various races and tribes) is an excellent example of how pseudo-scientific claims about "human races" shaped mainstream ideas of "race science" in nineteenth-century Switzerland. Schinz was also dedicated to publishing educational materials for schools, including *Der Kanton Zürich in naturwissenschaftlicher und landwirthschaftlicher Beziehung* (Science and agriculture in the canton of Zurich). This spirit of discovery in the surrounding regional wilderness of Zurich no doubt inspired Tschudi and Escher. During their youth, they co-founded the Okenia Verein, a society in honour of Lorenz Oken (1779–1851), a natural history professor and the first principal of the University of Zurich. Natural history, as learned by young Tschudi and Escher from Schinz, was a space for spreading patriotic ideas of the national wilderness as well as a racist discourse about cultural diversity.

When Tschudi decided to study under Professor Louis Agassiz—another problematic figure of natural history—in Neuchâtel, he broadened his academic training with his practice in the national territory. In Neuchâtel, Tschudi made his first scientific contributions to natural history with his publications about Swiss reptiles and the classification of batrachians. But his contribution to the Natural History Museum of Neuchâtel was not limited to Swiss fauna. Today, the Museum contains about 600 specimens gathered by Tschudi in Peru, one of the museum's largest collections. This unprecedented connection between the Peruvian rainforest and wealthy Neuchâtel is also illustrative of the global economic conjuncture that brought Tschudi to South America.

Tschudi set sail on 27 February 1838 from the port of Le Havre in the French ship *L'Edmond*. This voyage was organised by the Geneva-based Grenus banking family to introduce Swiss manufacturing to the world, sidestepping the intermediary costs of other commercial networks, especially those of the British. According to the original itinerary, the ship was to circumnavigate the world, rounding Cape Horn, then visiting Valparaíso, Mexico, the Aleutian Islands, and Kamchatka. At each port, Tschudi would be able to go hunting and collect specimens. The Coulon family of Neuchâtel, founders of the Natural History Museum, covered the expenses, sensing an opportunity to consolidate their museum's collections, whose original nucleus was Charles de Meuron's natural history cabinet. This cabinet contained the specimens collected by Meuron's regiment of mercenaries in the Dutch and British colonies. These Swiss mercenaries had an interest in rifles, gunpowder, and trade—as is evident in the collection in Neuchâtel—one that was shared subsequently by Tschudi in the Peruvian rainforest, via Neuchâtel. The material evidence of the stuffed animals served as the gateway through which imperial networks, trade aspirations, and scientific projects entered into the life of Swiss society.

Together with birds and monkeys, Tschudi brought back to Switzerland a diverse array of objects: Amerindian human remains and cultural artefacts considered "antiquities". The objects are today dispersed in Swiss museums, as well as in German and Austrian institutions. In recent years Tschudi's collections gained public attention because of the restitution of a statuette. Representing a deity called "Ekeko" by Indigenous people, the figure had been stolen by Tschudi from a sacred place in the Andean highlands in 1858 and was housed for more than a hundred years at the Historical Museum of Bern. It was finally returned to the Bolivian state in 2014 amid public controversy. Today, more objects from Tschudi's legacy in Swiss collections are under consideration for restitution; some of these are human remains, including mummified children. Carried out in the name of science, collecting is not a purely scientific quest. Gathering and safeguarding thousands of objects from all over the world have served as a means of hierarchising cultural diversity, with Europe and Switzerland at the top, and so legitimising a discourse of Western triumphalism.

→ fig. p.190

Diverted divinity

In 1858 the explorer Johann Jakob von Tschudi (1818–1889) stole a figure of the god Ekeko. The Historisches Museum in Bern returned it to Bolivia in 2015. This replica echoes the significance of the original.

Ekeko replica, sculpture, La Paz, 2020, Tomás Bartoletti, Zurich.

After Tschudi: The global traces of Swiss collections

To a certain extent, Tschudi's legacy is that of a pioneer of nineteenth-century Switzerland. Many other Swiss scientists followed in his footsteps later, but they did so in a variety of colonial contexts. Among the most renowned figures are Paul and Fritz Sarasin, who travelled to Sri Lanka (formerly British Ceylon) and to Sulawesi (formerly Celebes under Dutch control) in the late nineteenth century. The Sarasins are well known for their anthropological and ethnographic collections, which became the founding collections of the Ethnological Museum of Basel. As in the case of Tschudi, the large number of human remains and the Sarasins' studies on the "race" of the Weddas—studies which have been critically revised in recent years—were a milestone for Swiss society and the scientific community of the time.

→ fig. p. 267

Hans Schinz is another prominent example of scientific collecting and colonialism in the Swiss context. His position as professor of systematic botany, phytogeography, and botanical history at the university of Zurich and his role as director of the Zurich botanical gardens from 1895 to 1929 were the product of his journeys to the colonial territory of German South West Africa (now Namibia). His expedition brought back thousands of objects—plants, human remains, and ethnological artefacts—that filled university repositories. Like Tschudi and the Sarasins, Schinz was also dedicated to the study of "human races". As shown in his biography, collecting in colonial contexts offered opportunities to Swiss scientists to improve their reputations and, therefore, their careers.

There are numerous examples in Swiss history of scientific careers like the ones described above. The thousand objects from non-European contexts that fill Swiss museums and universities are evidence of such trajectories. These collections link Switzerland with Latin America, Africa, Asia, and Oceania, at times in unexpected ways. They prove how far Swiss scientists and missionaries travelled and how deeply they were entangled in European imperial networks. Nonetheless, the collections have helped to shape both an idea of cultural diversity based on racist assumptions and a natural order that deeply influenced the way Swiss society perceived other societies. To a certain extent, ideas of European supremacy, which Swiss museums have forged over years through those collections, served to ground global inequalities that have persisted into our own time.

Bartoletti, Tomás Joaquin: "Tschudi, Johann Jakob von" in *Historisches Lexikon der Schweiz* (HLS), in progress.

Bartoletti, Tomás Joaquin: "Masculine Knowledge and Natural History in Mid-Nineteenth Century: The Case of a Swiss Hunter in South America" in *Isis: Journal of the History of Science Association,* 116/1, 2021, pp. 1-25.

Bennett, Tony, Fiona Cameron and Nelia Dias: *Collecting, Ordering, Governing: Anthropology, Museums, and Liberal Government*, Durham, NC: Duke University Press, 2017.

Chambers, David Wade, and Richard Gillespie: "Locality in the History of Science: Colonial Science, Technoscience, and Indigenous Knowledge" in "Nature and Empire: Science and the Colonial Enterprise", *Osiris*, 15 (2000), pp. 221–240.

Coote, Anne, Alison Haynes, Jude Philp and Simon Ville: "When Commerce, Science, and Leisure Collaborated: The Nineteenth-Century Global Trade Boom in Natural History Collections" in *Journal of Global History*, 12/3, 2017, pp. 319–339.

Da Silva, Matheus Alves Duarte, Thomás A. S. Haddad and Raj Kapil (eds.): *Beyond Science and Empire: Circulation of Knowledge in an Age of Global Empires 1750–1945*, London: Routledge Taylor & Francis Group, 2024.

Finnegan, Diarmid A., and Jonathan Jeffrey Wright (eds.): *Spaces of Global Knowledge: Exhibition, Encounter and Exchange in an Age of Empire*, London: Routledge Taylor & Francis Group, 2015.

Findlen, Paula: *Possessing Nature: Museums, Collecting, and Scientific Culture in Early Modern Italy,* Berkeley: University of California Press, 1994.

Habermas, Rebekka, and Alexandra Przyrembel (eds.): *Von Käfern, Märkten und Menschen: Kolonialismus und Wissen in der Moderne*, Göttingen: Vandenhoeck & Ruprecht, 2013.

Häner, Flavio: *Dinge sammeln, Wissen schaffen: Die Geschichte der naturhistorischen Sammlungen in Basel 1735–1850*, Bielefeld: transcript, 2017.

Harrison, Simon: *Dark Trophies: Hunting and the Enemy Body in Modern War*, New York: Berghahn Books, 2012.

Schiebinger, Londa: "Forum Introduction: The European Colonial Science Complex" in *Isis* , 96/1, 2005, pp. 52–55.

MacGregor, Arthur: *Curiosity and Enlightenment: Collectors and Collections from the Sixteenth to the Nineteenth Century*, New Haven, CT: Yale University Press, 2007.

Pels, Peter: "The Anthropology of Colonialism: Culture, History, and the Emergence of Western Governmentality" in *Annual Review of Anthropology,* 26, 1997, pp. 163–183.

Quijano, Aníbal: "Coloniality of Power and Eurocentrism in Latin America" in *International Sociology*, 15/2, 2000, pp. 215–232.

Redman, Samuel J.: *Bone Rooms: From Scientific Racism to Human Prehistory in Museums*, Cambridge, MA: Harvard University Press, 2016.

Sarr, Felwine, and Bénédicte Savoy: *The Restitution of African Cultural Heritage: Toward a New Relational Ethics*, Paris: Philippe Rey/Seuil, 2018.

Schär, Bernhard Carlos, and Patrick Kupper (eds.): *Die Naturforschenden: Auf der Suche nach Wissen über die Schweiz und die Welt, 1800–2015*, Baden: Hier + Jetzt, 2015.

Schär, Bernhard Carlos: *Tropenliebe: Schweizer Naturforscher und niederländischer Imperialismus in Südostasien um 1900*, Frankfurt: Campus, 2015.

Schazmann, Paul-Emile: *Johann Jakob von Tschudi: Forscher, Arzt, Diplomat*, Zurich: Verlag Mensch und Arbeit, 1956.

Sheets-Pyenson, Susan: *Cathedrals of Science: The Development of Colonial Natural History Museums during the Late Nineteenth Century*, Montreal: McGill-Queen's, 1988.

Heesen, Anke te, and Emma Spary (eds.): *Sammeln als Wissen: Das Sammeln und seine wissenschaftshistorische Bedeutung*, Göttingen: Wallstein, 2001.

Brescius, Moritz von: *German Science in the Age of Empire: Enterprise, Opportunity and the Schlagintweit Brothers*, Cambridge: Cambridge University Press, 2018.

Paul Sarasin's telescope

Paul (1856–1929) and Fritz (1859–1942) Sarasin undertook several expeditions between 1883 and 1907. Using the most advanced measuring and recording equipment, they explored geological, geographical, and anthropological boundaries in Asia and Australia.

Extendable telescope in protective cover, c. 1900, Basel Historical Museum, photo: Alwin Seiler.

Headdress

The Zurich botanist and ethnographer Hans Schinz (1858–1941) conducted research and collected items between 1884 and 1997 in the colony of "German South-West Africa". This three-pointed leather hood with iron beads probably belonged to a married Herero woman from Omburu in what is today Namibia. Nothing else can be gleaned from the collector's notes.

Headdress, late nineteenth century, Ethnographic Museum at the University of Zurich, inv.no. VMZ 00214.

Two women unknown to us

Hans Schinz probably photographed these women in 1885. However, he treated them not as individuals with their own life stories, but as an "ethnographic category". On the strength of his colonial research in what is today Namibia, he received a professorship at the University of Zurich.

Herero women with leather headdress, photograph, Dr Hans Schinz, South-West Africa, c. 1885, Ethnographic Museum at the University of Zurich, inv. no. VMZ 395.01.011.

The exploitation of nature

Big-game hunting, plantation economy, and colonial climate impacts

Raphael Schwere

The European colonisation of the Americas had global consequences for the climate. In the century after the arrival of Christopher Columbus in the Bahamas in 1492, the world's surface temperature dropped by 0.15 degrees Celsius. According to a 2019 earth science study conducted by University College London, this change can be attributed to the fact that approx. 90 per cent of the Indigenous population was wiped out by diseases introduced to the Americas during this phase of colonisation as well as by colonial wars and the associated societal collapse. As a consequence, wide expanses of unused cultivated land reverted to forest. This new vegetation absorbed so much carbon dioxide that the reduction in greenhouse gases gave rise to what is known as the "Little Ice Age".

As in this early episode of colonial history, later colonial developments would have profound anthropogenic impacts on landscapes, flora, and fauna on every continent. These changes would likewise have an effect on the climate. The extent to which Swiss citizens were involved in the resulting exploitation of nature can be seen in the following two historical case studies and from examining the lasting impacts of these colonial ventures.

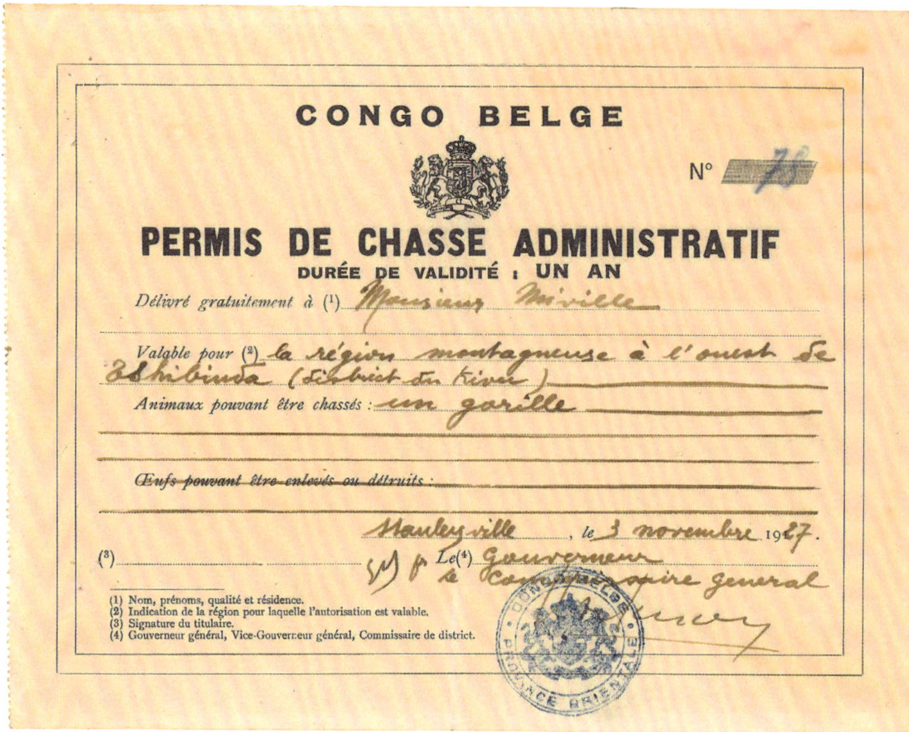

CONGO BELGE

N° 78

PERMIS DE CHASSE ADMINISTRATIF
DURÉE DE VALIDITÉ : UN AN

Délivré gratuitement à (1) Monsieur Miville

Valable pour (2) la région montagneuse à l'ouest de Tshibinda (district du Kivu)

Animaux pouvant être chassés : un gorille

~~*Œufs pouvant être enlevés ou*~~ *détruits :*

Stanleyville, *le* 3 novembre 1927.

(3) ....

Le(4) Gouverneur
le commissaire general

(1) Nom, prénoms, qualité et résidence.
(2) Indication de la région pour laquelle l'autorisation est valable.
(3) Signature du titulaire.
(4) Gouverneur général, Vice-Gouverneur général, Commissaire de district.

CONGO BELGE
PROVINCE ORIENTALE

Hunting permit

Hunting in the Belgian Congo was regulated by the colonial administration. A hunting licence issued to Eric Miville (1900–1967) from Basel illustrates this practice: in 1927, he obtained permission to shoot a gorilla in the Kivu region.

Hunting licence, Stanleyville (modern-day Kisangani), 1927, Burgerbibliothek of Bern, VA NHB 82.

Species extinction and how the "Animals of Africa" ended up in the museum

In 1923, the daughter-father duo Vivienne (1900–1957) and Bernard (1877–1924) de Watteville, descendants of the Wattenwyls, a wealthy Bernese patrician family, set out from their home in England on a "hunting safari" in East Africa. They had been commissioned to acquire exhibits for the Burgergemeinde Bern's Natural History Museum, and their contract also set out the distribution of the costs. The museum was responsible for transporting skins and bones to Bern, while the Wattevilles themselves took on the rest of the expedition expenses. Along with this scientific commission, they were also granted shooting permits by the colonial administration, which stipulated the animals that could be taken in colony territories according to region, species, age, sex, and numbers. An archived hunting licence issued to Eric Miville (1900–1967) of Basel in 1927 by the Belgian colonial administration for permission to shoot a gorilla in the region of Kivu sheds light on these types of arrangements. ← fig. p. 202

The permanent diorama exhibition "Animals of Africa" in Bern's Natural History Museum conveys an impression of the numerous animals brought down by the Wattevilles, most of them taken in British colonial territories. The spoil includes nineteen lions, the last of which managed to fatally wound Bernard de Watteville. Although his daughter was traumatised by the event, as we can glean from her 1927 memoir *Out in the Blue* (German title: *In blaue Fernen – Afrikanische Jagdabenteuer*), she continued her collecting activities. In late 1924 she discovered and killed a white rhinoceros, which she had been permitted to hunt, though the species was already under strict protection at the time. She wrote the following about this experience:

→ fig. p. 205

> There was no hazard about it, no beast alive is more docile than a white rhino, and no shooting poorer sport. The difficulty would be to find a good specimen, and much more, to remove the whole skin. Its bulk would be enormous, for rhino hide is thicker than elephant's.

Once it arrived at the museum, the rhinoceros was preserved and a diorama, a display case with trappings intended to imitate the animal's natural habitat, was constructed. From 1936 it was presented in the new museum building in Bern. As sociologist and science studies researcher Priska Gisler writes, the diorama communicated "perceptions of African landscapes devoid of people", which contributed to "an exoticisation of perceptions" of the African continent.

→ fig. p. 206

In reality, the African landscapes visited by colonial big-game safaris were not and are not devoid of people. The wildlife in these areas, however, was severely depleted. Vivienne de Watteville's "White Rhinoceros" belongs to the subspecies of the northern white rhinoceros. Today it is under

"Exotic" animals for the museum

In 1924, Vivienne de Watteville (1900–1957) killed a Northern White Rhino, one of the last living individuals of a species that was already in danger of extinction at the time. She was hunting on behalf of Bern's Natural History Museum, where the preserved rhino is still on display today. Museums collected and preserved what disappeared in the course of colonial expansion.

Vivienne de Watteville with white rhino, Uganda, 1924, Natural History Museum, Bern.

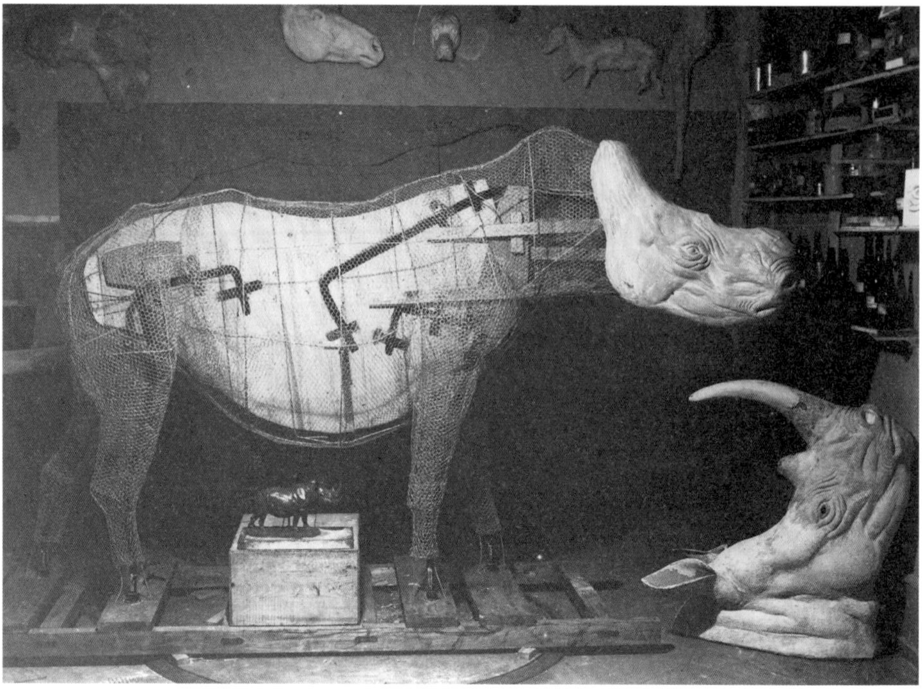

Image of Africa

The de Wattevilles killed countless animals in the territory of what is now Kenya and Uganda. From 1935/36 onward, they were preserved in the museum and presented in special display cases with idealised trappings. These “dioramas” shaped people’s ideas about the “savage” African continent.

Preparing the white rhino, Bern, between 1924 and 1935, Natural History Museum, Bern.

threat of extinction, and only two such animals are known to exist in the world. It can be said that the Wattevilles were collecting animals for the museum that disappeared over the course of colonial expansion.

The plantation as a colonial economic model

The plantation was an important scene of Swiss colonial history. Swiss plantation owners and managers could be found not only in the Americas but also on Sumatra, then part of the Dutch East Indies colony (1816–1949) and now part of Indonesia. Between the mid-nineteenth and the early twentieth centuries, up to a quarter of the Europeans in the Sultanate of Deli, the centre of the local plantation economy, held Swiss passports. From 1870 onwards, according to the historian Andreas Zangger, approximately 500 to 700 Swiss were working on plantations in East Sumatra after the Netherlands opened the area to European investment.

These individuals brought back a great number of photographs from Sumatra that are now held in the colonial archives of Swiss museums and that offer a glimpse of many aspects of the colonial plantation economy. The plantation economy was export-oriented, a fact that is illustrated, for example, by pictures of huge fermentation sheds with bales of tobacco ready for shipment. The selection of agricultural crops grown on a plantation was determined by whatever was in global demand at the time and fetched high prices, such as tobacco, rubber, or palm oil. Sumatra's plantations produced high-quality tobacco that was prized in Europe and America, and this tobacco was shipped to Switzerland to be processed into tobacco products.

Most of these photographs show people, both colonisers and colonised. The plantation economy depended on the latter as a cheap labour force that could carry out the physically demanding and unhealthy work. There were, and still are, massive social disparities between these workers and the plantation owners, disparities that were cemented by systems such as slavery, other forms of forced labour, and low wages. In the photos we also see clear examples of everyday colonial working relationships. They show the European management, Malay and indigenous Batak workers clearing the forest, Javanese planters, Chinese labourers processing raw materials, and people from the Indian subcontinent working, for example, as security guards or building streets and canals. The photographs show not only the existing racist hierarchies but also the exploitative and precarious working conditions which, according to historian Jürgen Osterhammel, could be likened to slavery.

Endangered biodiversity

Huge swathes of forest fell victim to Sumatra's plantation economy. The extensive interventions in nature were accepted in the interests of increasing the profits of colonial enterprises. Biodiversity decreased sharply—deforestation results in changes to the climate.

Beginning of a plantation: Clearing the forest, Sumatra, c. 1880–1900, Ethnographic Museum at the University of Zurich, inv. no. VMZ 528.00.030.

Resistance

This threatening letter, carved into a bamboo stick and addressed to Karl Fürchtegott Grob (1830–1893) of Zurich, bears witness to local resistance. The writer threatens to burn down a building if his conditions are not met.

Threatening letter with inscription in a Batak language, Sumatra, 1875–1880, Ethnographic Museum at the University of Zurich, inv. no. VMZ 01006.

Colonial exploitation of people went hand in hand with the overuse of nature. Plantations are large-scale monocultures that must be constantly expanded, and obtaining more and more fertile land was and is bound up with land conflicts and the destruction of habitat for flora and fauna—humans included. Land reclamation, achieved by clearing forests leased from the Malay sultans, often led to the theft of forest areas that were used and inhabited by Malays and Batak. The threatening letter written by a member of the Batak community to the Zurich-born plantation owner Karl Fürchtegott Grob (1830–1893) is an example of local resistance to the colonial plantation economy.

← fig. p. 209

← fig. p. 210

The colonial understanding of nature

In the albums of those who returned from Sumatra we find a surprising number of photographs documenting the clearing of primary forest. They give us an impression of the size and biodiversity of the forest areas that were replaced by plantations. The businesslike captions, such as "Clearing the virgin forest", "Beginning of a plantation: Clearing the forest", or "Cleared primeval jungle", are representative of the European plantation owners' understanding of nature. The radical changes to the landscape, flora, and fauna caused by the clearing, levelling, and digging of canals were viewed as necessary measures to increase the profits of colonial enterprises. The concept of the dualism of man and culture vs. nature that became widespread over the course of the Enlightenment developed into the idea, and even the ideal, of increasing people's knowledge of nature and its value as a resource. To some extent, this represented the secularisation of the Christian imperative to "fill the earth and subdue it". The colonial powers adopted this utilitarian motive to justify their appropriation and cultivation of land as well as the extraction and exploitation of all its resources, including the "primitive peoples".

These activities were also encouraged by the modern belief in progress. "More, bigger, faster, and further" was the goal. As European industrialisation led to an immeasurable growth in the demand for raw materials and a need to cover the immense costs of colonisation and colonial administration, the colonies served as a supposedly inexhaustible source of agricultural products, minerals, and labour.

Ecological (in)justice

The case studies from Swiss colonial history described above illustrate how Swiss citizens were involved in the colonial exploitation of nature. It is important to reappraise these histories, since the colonial structures make themselves felt to this day.

Today, colonial continuities are a global topic of public debate. In Switzerland, for example, the

Natural History Museum in Bern now offers its visitors a glimpse of research concerning the colonial history of its collections and dioramas. In Indonesia, the artist Maryanto introduces his own artistic research into the debate in the form of paintings and installations that offer a commentary on the entanglements of environmental exploitation and postcolonial sociopolitical structures. The 2023 work *Fresh Fruit Bunch* examines the rapid expansion of the palm oil plantation economy on Kalimantan (Borneo), the accompanying displacement of indigenous communities, and the destruction of the forest. The colonial economic model of the plantation, including its focus on export, environmental damage, and labour migration, is alive and well to this day. Only the cash crops, the saleable field crops, vary from one era to another. This agrarian model, which began in the territories of the former Swiss colonial plantations on Sumatra, is steadily expanding, and it continues to consume unused land. Today the Republic of Indonesia remains the world's largest producer of palm oil, the raw material which global companies use to produce food, cosmetics, and fuel. Alongside the dramatic effects on biodiversity, deforestation also contributes to the greenhouse effect, the "main driving force of climate change" according to the EU Commission's Climate Action department. The dense tropical forests that are being destroyed are huge, and the carbon dioxide they store is released into the atmosphere.

→ fig. p. 214/215

Maryanto

Fresh Fruit Bunch, Yogyakarta, 2023, acrylic on canvas.

Yeo Workshop, Singapore.

Palm oil fruit

The artist Maryanto is concerned with environmental exploitation and postcolonial structures in Indonesia. The picture of harvested palm oil fruit highlights the plantations on Kalimantan, the resulting displacement of Indigenous communities, labour migration, and forest degradation.

Sea level rise on the the coast of M'Bour, Senegal. Drone image, Khalifa Hussein, 2023.

Swiss National Museum.

Climate justice

Colonialism is one of the drivers of climate change. The former colonies bear the costs because they are more severely affected by its consequences. The footage of the flooded coast of Senegal by filmmaker Khalifa Hussein makes us aware of the urgency of the demand for climate justice.

The *Intergovernmental Panel on Climate Change* recognises two aspects of the relationship between colonialism and anthropogenic climate change: Colonialism is not only a driver of climate change, it is also responsible for the fact that the impact of climate change is particularly severe in the areas of the former colonies. According to data on global carbon dioxide emissions between 1750 and 2021, the world's formerly colonised regions, which now produce the least carbon dioxide, are the same areas that are bearing the brunt of climate change (for example, in the form of extreme heat, soil erosion, and rising sea levels). At the same time, the wealth generated by ecologically harmful economic practices for the most part benefits the Global North—including the former colonial powers—which has contributed more to carbon dioxide emissions and is seen as less susceptible to the effects of climate change today.

→ Jose Cáceres Mardones p. 255

This disparity is a topic of public discussion today and gives rise to calls for "climate justice". The re-evaluation of histories such as those of the Von Wattenwyl Collection or the Swiss plantations on Sumatra provide the historical underpinnings for this debate. And contemporary political artists like the Senegalese filmmaker Khalifa Hussein, who has documented the portentous results of rising sea levels on the coasts of his country using drone footage, help bring home the urgency of these demands for ecological justice.

← fig. p. 216

Bhattacharyya, Debjani: "Von den Anfängen des Anthropozäns: Was uns ins Zeitalter des Menschen geführt hat" in Sibylle Lichtensteiger and Anita Affentranger (eds.): *Natur: Und wir? Ein Buch über die entscheidende Frage unserer Zeit* (exhibition catalog), Stapferhaus Lenzburg, Basel, 2023, pp. 38–52.

Gisler, Priska: "Von Horizont zum Horizont: Das Löwendiorama im Naturhistorischen Museum Bern und seine koloniale Geschichte" in *Geschichte in Wissenschaft und Unterricht*, 74/9–10, 2023, pp. 533–549.

Intergovernmental Panel on Climate Change (ed.): *Climate Change 2022: Impacts, Adaptation, and Vulnerability,* Cambridge: Cambridge University Press, 2022.

Koch, Alexander, Chris Brierley, Mark M. Maslin, and Simon L. Lewis: "Earth System Impacts of the European Arrival and Great Dying in the Americas after 1492" in *Quaternary Science Reviews*, 207/1, 2019, pp. 13–36.

Li and, Tania, Pujo Semedi: *Plantation Life: Corporate Occupation in Indonesia's Oil Palm Zone,* Durham NC: Duke University Press, 2021.

Raja, Nussaïbah B.: "Colonialism Shaped Today's Biodiversity" in *Nature Ecology & Evolution*, 6, 2022, pp. 1597–1598.

Ritchie, Hannah, and Max Roser: "Per capita CO_2 Emissions", https://ourworldindata.org/co2-emissions#per-capita-co2-emissions (accessed 10 Oct. 2023).

Stoler, Ann Laura: *Capitalism and Confrontation in Sumatra's Plantation Belt 1870–1979,* New Haven, CT: Yale University Press, 1985.

Süess, Léonie: "Koloniales Erbe im Naturhistorischen Museum Bern", master's thesis, Zürcher Hochschule der Künste, Zurich, 2019.

de Watteville, Vivienne: *Out in the Blue*, London: Methuen, 1937.

Zangger, Andreas, and Ralph Harb: *Ferne Welten/Fremde Schätze: Ethnografische Objekte und frühe Fotografien aus Niederländisch-Indien*, Biel/Bienne: clandestin, 2020.

Colonialism and the institutionalisation of Swiss “racial research”

Marilyn Umurungi

When we consider phenomena such as racism and colonialism and how they relate to each other, it can certainly be constructive to start off by situating them in historical terms. Historians see European colonialism as having its roots in the fifteenth century, at the point when European powers started to expand their empires. Defining a point in history when racism began would mean specifying an exact date and place for when and where the phenomenon first appeared. But this is illusory, for two reasons. Firstly, there is no consensus among researchers about how "racism" is to be defined. Until the early 1970s, the dominant notions were based on a biological understanding of race, deriving from the assumption that there was such a thing as "human races". From the mid-1970s onwards, theories began to be formulated that outline an understanding of the phenomenon based on culture, increasingly categorising social and political discrimination on the basis of background, social class, religion, and gender as "racist". Secondly, if we examine the written sources produced by various peoples in prehistory and early history through to the modern era, hardly any of them allow us to deduce the extent to which racist thought and actions influenced their everyday lives. Sources are equally rare in cultures with predominantly oral traditions. Nonetheless, most historians approach the issue of how people in the ancient world viewed themselves and others as if they were exploring the inception of racism.

Us and the Others

What has repeatedly prompted historical research to surmise that the forms of political and social organisation of the modern era had a racist dimension is the development of an institution that goes back to the advanced civilisations of antiquity, namely slavery. It is almost impossible from a modern perspective to explain slavery, especially the transatlantic trade in enslaved people, without racism. Racism was an inherent aspect of both the exploitation and the control of human labour. But can this viewpoint, as shaped by a modern understanding of the concept of racism, also be applied to antiquity? In ancient Greece and Rome, enslaved people came from various social classes and regions, and so there would have been very little perception of a link between their enslavement and their respective cultural origins. For example, people were often enslaved after their side had been defeated in war, regardless of their original culture or social class.

There is, however, undeniably an asymmetrical (power) structure at play in the way that Greeks and Romans viewed their enemies and foreigners, specifically groups and peoples on the fringes of or beyond their spheres of dominance, from whom they abducted people into slavery after victorious battles. The decisive term in this context is "barbarian", an "asymmetrical antonym" to the Greeks' designation of themselves as "Hellenes". The conceptual relationship is asymmetrical above all in terms of its categorical distinction: "Hellene" was a proper name and denoted a particular cultural affiliation, while "barbarian" (which meant "incomprehensible") was an external ascription used generically to designate a supposed lack of culture. Greek historiography did indeed include honourable depictions of barbarians, but the term was primarily used for the normative devaluation of non-Greek cultures. Although the words "barbarian" and "Hellene" were clearly asymmetrical in relation to each other, it is not really possible to talk about the "beginning of racism" here either.

Using religion to preserve unity and difference

Religion was a decisive factor in producing classical, asymmetrical perceptual forms of cultural differences. The distinction between Christianity and Judaism, and later Islam too, played a particular role here at an early stage. And this can be clearly contextualised in history. Medieval Christian traditions contained two abstract elements that would become important for the later concept of "race", as it was articulated in particular during the era of European colonialism. Firstly, there was the concept of a "universal Christendom" and the associated idea of a global Christian community, allied with the notion that everything that might threaten and damage this

Christian community must be excluded or suppressed. This idea would later be incorporated into a scientised view of the world via the term "human races". The perceptions Christians had of themselves and others permitted both peaceful and violent forms of proselytising and (forced) conversion. That Jewish people were at risk within this structure had become apparent by the 1096 crusade at the very latest, when the first anti-Jewish pogroms and mass murders occurred. The kind of violent anti-Semitic racism that broke out at this point had never existed before.

In Switzerland, the first documented expulsions of Jews took place in the thirteenth century. The pogrom in the city of Bern in 1293 was triggered by the murder of a Christian boy, whose death was blamed on a Jewish money dealer called "Jöly (Joel)". The city's Grand Council decided not only to execute "Jöly" on the charge of child murder, but also to expel all the other Jews from the city, while an angry crowd destroyed the Jewish cemetery.

The characteristics of racism during colonialism

As Floris Biskamp explains, one of the reasons why researchers disagree about the definition of racism is that the subject matter itself has changed over the decades. Despite this dissent, most scholars researching racism assume that it was an intrinsic factor in legitimising an extreme form of exploitation and domination that emerged during European colonialism. One characteristic feature of "colonial racism" is that the exploitation was accompanied by the extensive disenfranchisement of racialised Others. A categorical, fundamental, and essential difference was constructed between the colonisers and the colonised, with the latter regarded either as inferior or not even as "proper" people. They were also thought to possess negative character traits and to be intellectually deficient and unable to determine their own lives. These ascriptions were supposedly scientifically justified by "biologist" theories which categorised various groups of people into "races"; this is ultimately the main feature of nineteenth-century "colonial racism".

Medicine as an instrument of standardisation

The "scientification" of racism and "racial theories" is often thought to have begun in the age of humanism. In the eighteenth century, a universal aspiration to enlightenment prevailed with respect to the natural and human sciences, represented by figures such as Jean-Jacques Rousseau (1712–1778) from Geneva and the Parisian philosopher Voltaire (1694–1778). The proponents of Enlightenment, with their monistic theories, became the "leading avant-garde of plans for social emancipation". The natural sciences, particularly medicine, were tasked with implementing reform. From then on, medicine was viewed as a science geared towards the common good—one that was intended to save humanity from its "deplorable state" and lead it to one that was "healthy". The Swiss psychiatrist and eugenicist Auguste Forel (1848–1931), for example, believed that this healthy state was the result of "natural selection", namely the superiority of "healthy" people over those who were "sick", thanks to the civilising achievements of medicine and "racial hygiene".

In the heyday of colonialism, arguments of this ilk allowed proponents of "racial hygiene" such as Auguste Forel, Eugen Bleuler (1857–1939), Hans Wolfgang Mayer (1882–1945), George Alexis Montandon (1879–1944), Otto Schlaginhaufen (1879–1973), and many others to spread their theories. Between 1892 and 1970, they subjected thousands of people classified by psychiatrists as "genetically inferior" to forced sterilisation in Zurich and Geneva, without any legal basis for doing so. What united these scientists was their desire to regulate and standardise individual (sexual) behaviour in order to achieve social control. The eugenicists in Switzerland were the European pioneers of "racial hygiene", a theory with its roots in the USA that aimed to eliminate "inferiors" from the *Volkskörper* or "national body".

Forel's student Alfred Ploetz (1860–1940) was one of the founders of "racial hygiene" in Germany. Another of his students, psychiatrist Ernst Rüdin (1874–1952), was among the leading "racial hygienists" in the Nazi era, while Rudolf Martin (1864–1925) from Zurich became one of the world's most influential anthropologists and pioneers of Swiss racial research.

From theory to institution

At the turn of the twentieth century, when Swiss anthropology first emerged in the scientific community of imperialist Europe, "racial science" was a heterogeneous field of research. It was the proponents of physical anthropology who would play a central part in its establishment, becoming experts in empirical questions about human development and how this had been presented by science over the course of the modern era. In particular, they investigated how human diversity could be explained by people's physical characteristics, lifestyles, and cultures.

Two new anthropological institutes in Switzerland took on a leading international role in this field of research: the Anthropological Institute at the University of Zurich and the Laboratoire d'Anthropologie at the University of Geneva. In Zurich, Rudolf Martin (1864–1925) stood out as one of the most ambitious "race researchers".

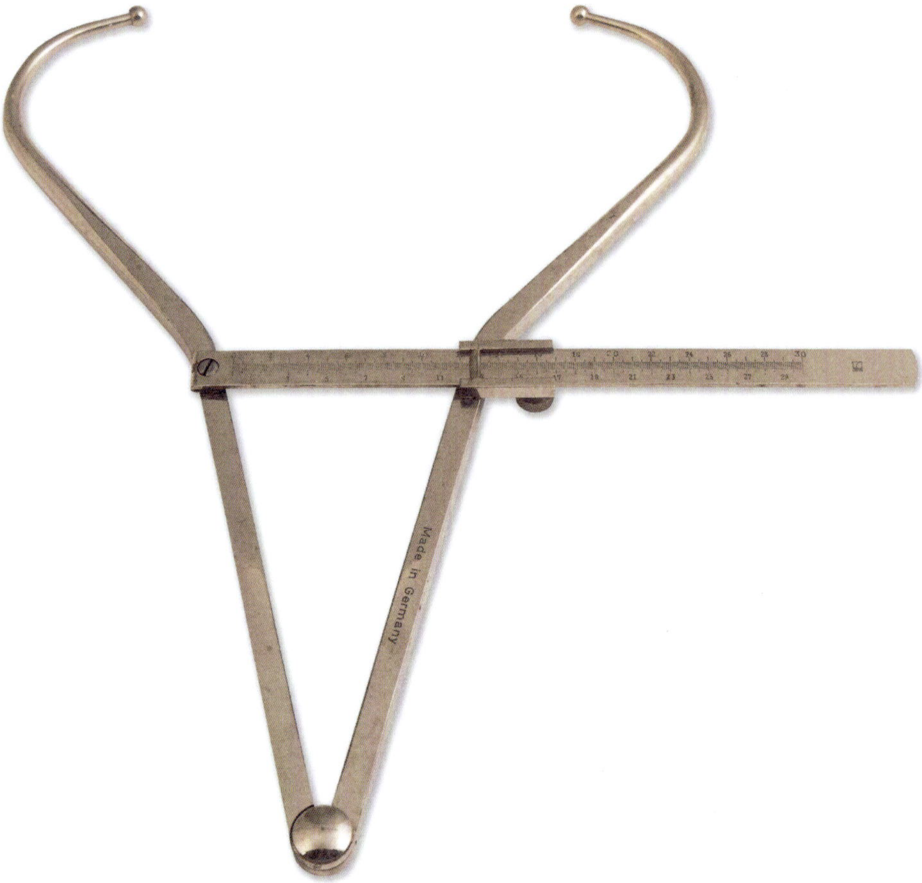

Instrument for measuring skulls

Callipers were the main instrument used for craniometry, that is, measuring skulls. In his anthropology textbook, Rudolf Martin (1864–1925) lists them alongside the technique of somatoscopy as an important aid for measuring the proportions of human and animal bodies.

Callipers, undated, Department of the History of Medicine at Bern University.

Among other things, his 1897 study *Ziele und Methoden einer Rassenkunde der Schweiz* (Aims and methods of racial anthropology in Switzerland) provided the first overview of the state of physical anthropology in the country. Although the first studies on the craniology of the Swiss population had already been published in the 1860s, it was only in 1899, when Martin was appointed chair of anthropology—which had been established specifically for him—that large-scale anthropological studies were carried out on living people: for example, by investigating the eye, skin, and hair colour of schoolchildren in the canton of Bern. From 1916 onwards in Geneva, Eugène Pittard (1867–1962) compiled the first-ever overviews of "racial forms" in the Swiss population with respect to their anthropological composition and statistics by looking at a measurable characteristic, namely height. The techniques and instruments developed by Martin and his students for carrying out measurements formed a globally applicable "kit" for the (anthropo)metric identification of "racial differences" in the first half of the twentieth century and would prove of central importance in scientising and institutionalising "racial theory". The Anthropological Institute in Zurich influenced anthropometric methodology at a global level more than any other institution.

← fig. p. 228

As Pascal Germann notes, when Swiss racial research emerged it was subject to the "epistemic and political conditions of European imperialism and benefited from this when the demand for racial anthropological expertise increased in 1930s Europe, which was becoming ever more dominated by fascists". It is remarkable that even after 1945, at a time when "racial research" was facing increasing criticism outside Switzerland, the anthropological institutes in Geneva and Zurich, far from losing their international reputation, were if anything viewed even more positively. Unlike in Germany, the concepts and procedures developed here in the name of "racial theory" were regarded as the "guarantors of objective, politically neutral research" because they came from a neutral country without colonies. As a result, they seemed particularly suitable as a continued means of lending scientific authority to "racial theory". Swiss racial research reached a peak in the first decade after the war and only became less important towards the end of the 1950s.

The others and us

← Marina Amstad p.79

As Marina Amstad's essay on everyday life in Switzerland shows, ideas about goods, property, and "race" were linked in new ways by the emergent consumer culture. At the turn of the twentieth century, there was a shift from "scientific racism" to "commodity racism". The general population accessed colonial images, fantasies, and thought patterns through the dissemination of advertising, magazines, "human zoos", and exhibitions. However, communicating the concept of European superiority went beyond popular culture. Racist discourses were also constructed and reproduced in science and religious education by means of written and illustrated learning materials and games.

In conclusion, the theories on supposed differences between "human races" that evolved from the scientification and institutionalisation of racial research contributed to various kinds of racisms and stereotypes becoming entrenched in the minds of numerous people during the age of colonialism and beyond.

Biskamp, Floris: "Rassismus, Kultur und Rationalität: Drei Rassismustheorien in der kritischen Praxis" in *Peripherie*, 37/146–147, 2017, pp. 271–296, https://doi.org/10.3224/peripherie.v37i2.07 (accessed 14 Nov. 2023).

Geulen, Christian: *Geschichte des Rassismus*, Munich: C.H. Beck, 2021, pp. 14–45.

Germann, Pascal: "Abschied vom Homo Alpinus: Zur Geschichte der Schweizer Rassenforschung in globaler Perspektive" in Jovita dos Santos Pinto et al. (eds.): *Un/Doing Race: Rassifizierung in der Schweiz*, Zurich: Seismo, 2022, pp. 225–248.

Purtschert, Patricia: *Kolonialität und Geschlecht im 20. Jahrhundert*. Bielefeld: transcript, 2012, pp. 77–88.

Querner, Hans: "Zur Geschichte der Anthropologie" in *Anthropologischer Anzeiger*, 44/4, 1986, pp. 281–297.

Staub, Kaspar: *Der biologische Lebensstandard in der Schweiz seit 1800*, inaugural dissertation at the University of Bern's faculty of philosophy and history, Bern: Selbstverlag, 2010, pp. 94–140.

Stereotypical constructs

The stereotypical portrayals of Black people in advertising for dirt-removing or bleaching cleansers as well as toothpastes were widespread between the 1920s and 1950s, revealing the construct that “White = clean” and “Black = dirty” in historical racial discourse.

Uhu-Line, poster, Theo Ballmer, printed by Wassermann W. Graph. Anstalt, Basel, undated, Swiss National Museum.

Controversial scientist

Jean Louis Rodolphe Agassiz (1807–1873) achieved world renown with his work on classification and historical geology as well as for founding the discipline of glaciology. Today his work is criticised because it implicitly supported the scientification of racist ideologies.

Jean Louis Rodolphe Agassiz, carte de visite, William Shaw Warren, c. 1865, HUP Agassiz, Louis (26A), Harvard University Archives.

Sasha Huber

Rentyhorn Sign, 2008, engraved aluminium on wood, 31.5 × 33 cm.

Collection of the Museum of Contemporary Art Kiasma, Helsinki.

Demounting Agassiz

The Rentyhorn sign is part of the ongoing multimedia campaign Demounting Louis Agassiz, which was initiated in 2007 by artists and activists under the leadership of historian Hans Fässler.

The aim of the campaign was to rename the Agassizhorn in the canton of Bern, but this was rejected by the decisive municipalities.

The changing perspectives at museums

Archival coloniality and restitution debates

Esther Tisa Francini

With its more than 1,000 museums and some 77 million works, Switzerland ranks among the countries with the highest museum density. Its archival and library landscapes are equally diverse. The various collections came into existence in very different ways and can be read from different angles. Of late, there has been increasing scrutiny of the extent to which imperialistic practices of rule, along with colonial oppression, exploitation, and appropriation, are reflected in Swiss collections, and how far Swiss actors benefited from European colonial systems. Indeed, the numerous collections, archives, and knowledge resources point to successful trade relations, a politically stable centre, and the financial means that made this kind of enrichment possible in the first place. At the same time, they provide evidence of curiosity and passion, of global interdependencies and entanglements, and of institutional power.

Re-reading the archives

When Swiss archives and their contexts of origin are viewed in their transnational dimension, new insights emerge into museum history, exhibition narratives, and the presentation of exhibits. The focus here is on provenance, that is, on the history of the origin and transfer of works as well as all the legal and ethical issues surrounding ownership. Against the background of globalisation

Butterflies from the colonies

Heinrich Escher (1776–1853), father of Alfred Escher, traded in land, cotton and colonial goods in America. He was also involved in a coffee plantation with enslaved people in Cuba. During his time overseas, he collected butterflies and insects. His 66,000 specimens are the founding collection of the Swiss Federal Polytechnic (now the Swiss Federal Institute of Technology Zurich, or ETH Zurich for short).

Lepidoptera from the collection of Heinrich Escher, donation, 1858, ETH Zurich, Entomological Collection.

and digitisation and under the new legal definition of museums adopted in 2022, inclusion and diversity are the order of the day. This translates into a plural perspective, a heterogeneity that goes hand in hand with various "gestures of showing" (Muttenthaler/Wonisch), a new accessibility to archives, an awareness of the "shared heritage", and new ethical relationships with the formerly colonised or dominated societies of origin (Sarr/Savoy).

Many museums have holdings that betray a colonial influence or emerged during the colonial era. They include zoological, anthropological, and botanical collections, artefacts from non-Western cultures, photographs, and manuscripts. These may be held in history museums, university archives, art museums, ethnographic museums, or even local museums.

← fig. p. 240

In recent years, the history of collections and museums has received a new lease of life from the approaches adopted by postcolonial studies and provenance research, the latter of which has further evolved on the basis of studies of cultural assets seized as a result of persecution under National Socialism (Tisa Francini/Csernay). Looking beyond the orientation and discipline of the individual museums and perceiving those institutions as archives assembled by people with diverse interests yields new insights into the collections. Archives are instruments of power that not only tell of the presence of history but also speak of its absence. In Swiss museum archives, there is little to be found about the colonial acquisition contexts of art and thus about the circumstances in which objects were removed from their original context. And that makes for an extremely one-sided perspective.

The change of perspective in museums is bringing to light themes and voices that until now have received little attention. Four examples illustrate the extent to which colonial history is linked to the collections, how differently the archives can be read, what kind of knowledge is imparted and what culture of remembrance thereby cultivated, and, finally, what scenarios and challenges may arise in the future.

Exhibiting: Dealing with sensitive artefacts

Mummies and their coffins found their way into Swiss collections in the nineteenth and early twentieth centuries. For the past two decades, the Swiss Coffin Project has been drawing together information on these exhibits from across Switzerland and making them accessible. Like the Benin Initiative Switzerland (see below) and, much more broadly, the Digital Benin website, this attempt to create a national network for cataloguing and research ensures the visibility and comparability of object types or objects from a specific art region; and that is important for the general cataloguing of and research into cultural assets. While the mummies and their coffins are often a huge attraction at museums, they may cause unease.

In November 2022, the Shep-en-Isis mummy from the St. Gallen Abbey Library made headlines thanks to an initiative by the theatre director and writer Milo Rau called the "St. Gallen Declaration for Shep-en-Isis". It was the first time that a call was made for the mummy to be repatriated to Egypt—in other words, to be removed from the place where it has been exhibited for some 200 years as a "curiosity", a highlight in the library of a baroque monastery. In previous centuries, libraries were simultaneously cabinets of curiosities in which a whole range of object types were collected, demonstrating relationships, knowledge, and power in equal measure.

It was amid the "Egyptomania" of the nineteenth century that the Shep-en-Isis mummy with its two coffins ended up in St. Gallen, the first mummy to arrive in Switzerland. While there are very few sources that allow us to reconstruct the excavation and sale of Shep-en-Isis, it is said that the mummy and its coffins were sent in 1820 to the governing magistrate of St. Gallen, Karl Müller-Friedberg, by his old school friend Philipp Roux, a merchant then living in Alexandria. At that time, Egypt was ruled by Pasha Muhammad Ali; it had not been colonised by a European country and export bans were unknown. Egypt passed a corresponding law in 1835 and began establishing a state collection in 1840.

Müller-Friedberg gave Shep-en-Isis to the Abbey Library as a loan immediately after the mummy's arrival in the country. The sale was concluded in 1836, and Shep-en-Isis has been one of the institution's main attractions ever since. These circumstances—and especially the presentation of the mummy as an object of spectacle—must be discussed. Beyond the provenance and history of the transfer, which bears the stamp of imperialism, there has been a recurring sense of unease about the mummy. Where does it belong? How should it be exhibited? What is being said about it?

Returning artefacts: Indigenous perspectives

Not long after the arrival of the mummy, a small stone figure from Bolivia found its way to Switzerland in 1858. It was brought into the country in the luggage of the Swiss explorer, linguist, and diplomat Johann Jakob Tschudi (1818–1889) together with many other objects, including hundreds of animal specimens, which are now held at the Natural History Museum in Neuchâtel.

← Tomás Bartoletti p. 181

Tschudi spent several years in Latin America in three separate stints, researching fauna and flora, collecting a huge number of specimens, and writing numerous books. His scientific achievements also include taxonomies and linguistic studies. However, his extensive writings are riddled with racist attitudes and thus bear stark witness to unequal power relations. The importance of science in entrenching world views can scarcely be overestimated. In this sense, it is legitimate to regard Swiss researchers in (post)colonial structures as political.

Tschudi himself recorded in writing how he had extorted the small stone figure from the inhabitants of Tiwanaku after getting them drunk—a trick that testifies to both his mania for collecting and the lengths he would go to in order to get what he wanted. There are important ruins at Tiwanaku, which were plundered many times, not least at the beginning of the twentieth century. In 2000, Tiwanaku was declared a UNESCO World Heritage Site.

The small stone deity—at times referred to as "Ekeko" by the indigenous people—remained in the Tschudi family for a good three-quarters of a century. In 1929, the Bern History Museum purchased the object for inclusion in its ethnographic collection. ← fig. p.190

In 2014, the museum returned the deity to the Bolivian National Museum of Archaeology in La Paz. By then, the stone figure had been on display in Bern for almost a century. What stories were told in connection with it? What was its significance for the museum, for Bern, for Switzerland? The work is regarded as part of the cultural heritage of humanity, which, as long as it was in Tschudi's collection in Bern, symbolised the history and the cultures of the Andes. Following its

Provenance research clarifies and publishes the origin and change of ownership of collection objects. The following chronology is documented for this bracelet:

18th/19th century: Royal Guild ofivory carvers at the court of Benin, originator, Benin City

18th/19th century: Royal Guild of Ivory Carvers at the Court of Benin, originator, Benin City

1888: Oba Ovonramwen (c. 1857–1914), Benin City

1897: Sir Harry Rawson (1843–1910), Commander-in-Chief of the British Army, Benin City, looted [1]

before 1968: Han Coray (1880–1974), collector, circumstances of acquisition unknown [2]

presumably 1974: Hans Coray (1906–1991), collector, acquired by inheritance

presumably 1985: Hans W. Kopp (1931–2009) [3]

2001: Museum Rietberg, purchased from Hans W. Kopp [4]

Proof of provenance

[1] Cf. Felix von Luschan, *Die Altertümer von Benin,* 1919, p. 399 with illustration. It is unclear until when the object remained in the possession of Harry Rawson or possibly his heirs. See Staatsbibliothek Berlin, Nachlass Felix von Luschan, box 17, letter from Admiral Rawson to Felix von Luschan 15 August 1901; British Museum Archive, AOA, Correspondence between C.H. Read and Felix von Luschan/ C.H. Read and Captain George Egerton, 1901–1903.

[2] Number on inside page (Reg. No. EA1?)

[3] Archive Museum Rietberg, folder "Eingangsdokumente, Ausgaben-Anweisung zum Ankauf, 14.11.2001 und Ebd. S.0002-0016, Rechnung RAF 608 & 609".

[4] Cf. Archive Museum Rietberg, Inventory book IV/157.

Bracelet from the Kingdom of Benin

This ivory bracelet was published in the extensive work *Die Altertümer von Benin* (1919) by Felix von Luschan. General Harry von Rawson, who was mainly responsible for the destruction and looting of the city of Benin in 1897, is named as the owner.

Bracelet adorned with a horseman and animal figures, Ikoo akon'eni, Edo, 18th/1st half of the 19th century, Ivory, Museum Rietberg, Inv.-No. RAF 608, Photo: Rainer Wolfsberger.

return to its native land, the deity is certain to have undergone a process of revalorisation and revitalisation, ultimately leading to a reassessment of its cultural heritage status.

The question arises as to whether the appropriation of "Ekeko" was an exception or typical of Tschudi's modus operandi. Tschudi not only transferred objects but also produced knowledge for Europe, albeit knowledge that was new only to the Europeans; it was not new for the Bolivians, who were deprived of access to that knowledge through his acquisitions. Thus, the colonisation of Latin America, in particular, which freed itself from Spanish rule at the beginning of the nineteenth century, was continued through science.

Collaborative provenance research: Dialogue and the future of the objects

The Benin Initiative Switzerland brings together eight public museums in Switzerland. Since 2021, it has been focusing on around 100 works from the Kingdom of Benin. Based on the approach of collaborative provenance research, the participating institutions, together with Nigerian partners, are investigating the significance and provenance of the objects and the stories behind them. The search for the royal works of art, mostly made of brass, ivory, or terracotta, some of them demonstrably and others very probably looted

← fig. p. 246

by the British in 1897, began in the holdings and archives of the museums and was then extended to colonial archives, the estates of dealers, auction and exhibition catalogues, and public archives. Oral history, especially that gleaned in Benin City, about issues such as how to date objects and establish both their function and their historical, cultural, and, not least, symbolic and religious value were another productive line of inquiry.

Even if the routes along which the works reached Switzerland cannot be fully reconstructed in each case, there are questions to be answered. Just over half of the objects fall into the category of looted or possibly looted works, for which courses of action are now under consideration. In a joint declaration at the beginning of February 2023, representatives from the Royal Palace in Benin City and from Nigerian state museums, universities, and artists' guilds agreed with the Swiss museum directors that ownership of these objects should be transferred. Ultimately, the decisions will be made by the trustees of the museums, be they cities, cantons, or foundations, given the fact that restitution always touches on sociopolitical issues.

Many of these works, which are central to the history of the royal palace, must be regarded as archives of knowledge, while others are cultural symbols or hold spiritual significance in the context of ancestor worship. Because Benin was robbed of its history in 1897 and the visual archive is not available in the local setting, it is essential to engage in dialogue and forge a joint solution for the future; in this way, knowledge and history can be shared and objects can be reclassified for future use.

Remembering: Artistic research

Over and above questions related to the historical context of collections, provenance research, and restitution, artists are engaging with colonial archival holdings, in light of to their own background or simply because they are interested in such holdings.

The Algerian-French artist Kader Attia supports the artistic recovery of stolen history as well as abducted and misappropriated art. He is interested in scarring, repairs, and recontextualisations, as evidenced by an exhibition at the Kunsthaus Zürich in 2020 and the works that have entered the museum's collection. Swiss artist Uriel Orlow takes archives as the starting point in his search for the traces of colonialism. He explores the legacy of colonialism in Switzerland and regards "nature as a witness to history"; in 2008—at the same time as the major Benin exhibition, which was shown in Vienna, Berlin, and Chicago—he artistically explored the overthrow of the kingdom of Benin by the British in 1897. The Franco-Congolese artist and lecturer Michèle Magema has processed her family history by approaching and appropriating the Hans Himmelheber Archive—for example, in the exhibitions *Fiction Congo* and *Look Closer* at the Museum Rietberg (2019–20 and 2023, respectively). Today, the Museum Rietberg is updating its holdings, some of which were acquired by collectors and dealers during the colonial era, by incorporating the works of contemporary artists; in this way, it addresses both the history of colonialism and how collections come into being. In *Voices of an Archived Silence*, the Sri Lankan artist Deneth Piumakshi Veda Arachchige explores the coloniality of archives. Her work enriched the exhibition *Thirst for Knowledge Meets Collecting Mania* at the Museum der Kulturen Basel (2019–20).

→ fig. p. 267

Shaping the future together

On the one hand, the large number of Swiss collections reflects the financial power of the collecting institutions and private individuals as well as the importance of the economic, scientific, and cultural appropriation of tangible and intangible cultural assets. On the other, it points to the global interdependencies of Switzerland and thus, indirectly, the role played by the Swiss in colonisation. And this means that the numerous, extensive, and, above all, very diverse collections also tell the story of the colonial entanglement of Swiss researchers, merchants, missionaries, diplomats, and museums.

It will be essential to continue to discuss the legality of colonial collections and their legitimacy in Switzerland. The complex biographies of the actors, the tortuous routes along which objects were transferred, and the ways in which museums present and describe their exhibits must all be examined and brought up to date. Because history cannot be undone, it demands a critical approach. This can take various forms, mediated not least through the diversity of exhibitions, through shifts in perspective, through the jointly researched and curated presentation of objects, and through the transfer of ownership and the return of objects.

Even though restitution has always been a political issue, the question of handing back objects should not be decided by politics alone (Goldmann/Loewenstein). In particular, the example of the Benin Initiative Switzerland shows how dialogue can be part of the debate about our shared cultural heritage from the outset. The aim is not to play off the European legal system against others, but to complement prevailing law in order to find viable ways to go about re-reading the archives today. Numerous considerations, which also underpin the ethical guidelines of the International Council of Museums (ICOM), need to be discussed while also addressing the significance of cultural assets from all periods and places.

Given the vast size of museum holdings, which are a long way from having been fully catalogued, much less researched, the museums must reflect on the collection concepts they have been using and whether they still make sense today. The act of “collecting” stands for passion, curiosity, and knowledge as well as power, appropriation, and enrichment. Problematising the term is the order of the day. Above all, the discussion on the colonial nature of collections is an endeavour that relates to history, the future of the past, and memory in the present.

Restitution should be regarded not as a loss but as a gain. Museums should provide a forum that allows for various interpretations and facilitates the restructuring of both object and knowledge collections. The question of the coloniality of Swiss archives represents an important contribution to any critical discussion about museum narratives and the presentation of exhibits, about global cooperation and returns, and, finally, about the democratisation and decentralisation of perspectives.

"Dekoloniale Prozesse an Schweizer Hochschulen und Kulturinstitutionen" in *TSANTSA: Zeitschrift der Schweizerischen Ethnologischen Gesellschaft,* 24, 2019.

Ebeling, Knut: "Mal d'Archives Revisited or Archive Evils from a Postcolonial Perspective: An Obstructed View" in Carl Deussen and Yagmur Karakis: *Thinking About the Archive & Provenance Research,* boasblog papers 4, Bonn, Bremen, Colgen, Siegen: boasblogs, 2022, pp. 8–14.

Goldmann, Matthias and Beatriz von Loebenstein: "Alles nur geklaut? Zur Rolle der juristischen Provenienzforschung bei der Restitution kolonialer Kulturgüter" in *MPIL Research Papers*, 2020–19, 2020.

Gonseth, Marc-Olivier, Jacques Hainard, and Roland Kaehr (eds.): *Le Musée cannibale*, Neuchâtel: Museum of Ethnography, 2002.

Jallo, Zainabu (ed.): *Material Culture in Transit: Theory and Practice*, London: Routledge, 2023.

Muttenthaler, Roswitha and Regina Wonisch: *Gesten des Zeigens: Zur Repräsentation von Gender und Race in Ausstellungen*, Bielefeld: transcript, 2006.

Plankensteiner, Barbara (ed.): *Benin: Geraubte Geschichte*, Berlin: Hatje Cantz, 2023.

Pomian, Krzysztof: *Le Musée: Une histoire mondiale*, vol. 3, *À la conquête du monde, 1850–2020*, Paris: Gallimard, 2022.

Sarr, Felwine and Bénédicte Savoy: *Zurückgeben: Über die Restitution afrikanischer Kulturgüter*, Berlin: Matthes & Seitz, 2019.

Tisa Francini, Esther, in cooperation with Sarah Csernay (eds.): *Wege der Kunst – Wie die Objekte ins Museum kommen*, Zurich: Scheidegger & Spiess, 2022.

Wallmapu, Ayiti,
and Abya Yala

Inequality and exploitation
in the Global South

Jose Cáceres Mardones

"Do you see what you have done and continue to do?" This was what Guaman Poma de Ayala asked of no less a figure than the Spanish king Philip III in the early seventeenth century. Guamán Poma was criticising not only the negative changes that the Spanish colonial regime had wrought upon Inca society, but also the long-term consequences of the colonial system in general. He repeatedly invoked the figure of his son for the purpose. What kind of society would his son be able—or forced—to live in Peru? Today, Guaman Poma's question could be put to many others, too: transnational corporations, legislators, G7 states, international organisations, and the presidents of countries—both in the Global North and the Global South. Addressing the ramifications of colonialism is still a relevant issue. Indeed, independence and decolonisation by no means brought an end to colonial structures in Latin America, Africa, and Asia. The territories colonised in the past, which we refer to as the Global South, are still marked by inequality and exploitation, and these consequences are manifested, revealed, and entrenched in their structures.

Post-colonialism, coloniality, and the double fracture

Postcolonialism never meant that colonialism had ceased to exist. The structures that emerged directly out of colonialism are testament to this. It is a situation that affects Switzerland, too: the country's cultural attitudes and material circumstances are simply a postcolonial reverberation. In this respect, postcolonial theory has become a useful discourse in the Global North, not only for relativising difficult concepts such as imperialism and neocolonialism but also for harmonising the past and present. Postcolonialism paradoxically underpinned the invisibility of the groups it was supposed to represent. Actors and theorists from the Global South have begun to criticise these kinds of constructions and develop new concepts and theoretical approaches that better reflect the prevailing realities and are based on the Global South's historical and material contexts. The following considerations and explanations relate specifically to Latin American decolonial theory.

The Peruvian sociologist Aníbal Quijano coined the analytical term "coloniality" to describe the inequality of (post)colonial societies. According to Quijano, the emergence of modernity goes hand in hand with the conquest of America because the latter was based on the unequal treatment of people, which is what allowed the capitalist system to take hold. "Race" thus becomes the basic principle that structures modernity, a context described

← Marilyn Umurungi p. 219

by Quijano as the "coloniality of power". Moreover, this coloniality is characterised by a corresponding kind of knowledge, namely a "modern" epistemology that produces and keeps on reproducing these differentiations. These kinds of hierarchies continue to grow in the realm of being. The consequences of colonialism in the Global South should thus be understood as persistent formations that have to be analysed within their historical and geographical contexts.

A further epistemological tool in this context is "decolonial ecology" as postulated by Malcom Ferdinand. His critique of modernity is linked to a critique of past and present-day environmental discourse, based on a simultaneous ecological and colonial divide that he calls the "double fracture of modernity". The ecological fracture results from the dualism between nature and culture, while the colonial fracture is based on the distinction and demarcation between "us" (civilised, modern, developed) and "them" (uncivilised, non-modern, underdeveloped), serving to legitimise the imperial quest for possession.

These foundations of coloniality are based on an inequality among humans as well as between nature and humans. They establish a system of practices that can be informal or formal, private or public, and situate exploitative and ecocidal phenomena in the Global South.

Wallmapu

Although Chilean revolutionaries declared their country's independence in 1810, political freedom did not change the make-up of coloniality as described above because it was a complex system that had influenced the mentality of the Latin American Creole activists and fighters, who based their rights on factors such as their Spanish ancestry. In addition, the Latin Americans fighting for independence had been inspired by the French Revolution and were accordingly informed by a European manner of thinking. The "coloniality of power" based on "race", as Quijano describes it, was neither questioned nor corrected. On the contrary, it actually formed the basis for state-building, as exemplified by the Chilean state and its treatment of the Indigenous Mapuche people.

Wallmapu was the territorial home of the Mapuche even before the new republic and the subsequent state of Chile came into existence. As an entity that encompasses both tangible and intangible aspects, Wallmapu is more than just a physical, geographical place; it is a living being where various creatures coexist and make life possible. In geographical terms, Wallmapu extends from the Limarí River in the north to the island of Chiloé in the south, incorporating territory on the eastern side of the Andes. To use contemporary terminology, Wallmapu could thus be described as a transnational area situated between Chile and Argentina. This is where the Mapuche live, although they cannot inhabit the territory in accordance with the above propositions because the Chilean state has enacted various laws to promote the abolition of collective land ownership. An arbitrary legal process has been implemented in this respect that progressively deprives those who are legally recognised as Mapuche of their rights. This situation is developing within the racist structures established by colonialism.

It should be noted that the Spanish crown recognised the autonomy of the Mapuche from 1641 onwards. The land was only divided up again after Chile and Argentina had emerged as nation states in the nineteenth century, with partitions that would not have been possible without violent military occupation. The Mapuche lost not only their autonomy but also most of the territory which they had once controlled. Their land was occupied by Chilean, German, and Swiss settlers, restricting their access to natural resources, which in turn altered the diversified character of the Mapuche economy, drove the Indigenous population into poverty and forced them apart, and ultimately led to the fragmentation of Mapuche social life in Wallmapu.

The Mapuche people were subjected to a process of racist denigration, with negative attributions that made it possible to control, steer, and regulate the Wallmapu region and its inhabitants. While they had been portrayed as warlike and disloyal in the first few centuries of the colony, in the new Chilean state they were depicted as uncivilised, lazy alcoholics. Colonialism is an epistemological project, too: the knowledge produced in chronicles, relationships, treaties, reports, and so on was used as another means of conquest in order to damage and control the image of Wallmapu. Even today, the Mapuche are still fighting against this construct, which restricts their scope of action.

Ayiti

Haiti was the first Black republic and the first territory in Latin America and the Caribbean to gain independence. These days, the country is better known for its political instability and chronic poverty. A little-known fact concerns the extensive deforestation that gives Haiti its current appearance. In a country that consists of 25 per cent flatland and 75 per cent mountains, the Food and Agriculture Organization of the United Nations estimated in 2015 that only 3.5 per cent of Haitian territory was covered in forest. Yet according to calculations by Gérard and Mimi Barthélemy, 80 per cent of the island was forested when Columbus landed there. When Haiti declared its independence in 1804, following three centuries of Spanish and French colonisation, a large part of the plains had probably already been cleared to make way for sugar cane and indigo plantations.

Although the most recent studies actually estimate that a full 30 per cent of the country is forested, acute deforestation and soil erosion continue to be a direct consequence of colonialism. It cannot be denied that the colonisation of the island laid the foundations for dealing with nature: it is there to serve humans and is subordinate to them. These circumstances illustrate how colonial conditions affect the country's landscape and contribute to climate change. At the same time, the country's environmental policy takes an approach to deforestation that illustrates the continuing colonial hierarchies.

Any technical, objective depiction of this situation begins as a story without people; it is about quantifying the catastrophe. Such a view rarely reveals the violence committed against the human and non-human actors who suffer from the consequences of deforestation and bioerosion. When people do appear in such reports, they are contained within the hierarchies of coloniality. Escaped slaves known as Maroons were held responsible for deforestation, along with farmers. The Maroons had run away from the slave plantations and sought refuge in the mountains, where they cleared parts of the forest to build shelters. By contrast, the farmers cultivated the steep slopes because soil erosion had made the valley floors unproductive. However, the limited arable land meant that yields were low, and so they supplemented their income by felling trees to produce

← Raphael Schwere p. 199

charcoal, which they then sold in town. This deforestation by various groups is closely linked to their (colonial) living conditions: they were exploited for their labour and economically marginalised. The slavery and soil erosion that fuelled their actions were a causal consequence of the colonial system, whereby enslaved people and land were exploited for the plantations. Yet, today, deforestation and its consequences are blamed on the Maroons and—in particular—on the farmers.

Potential solutions proposed so far have been based on the same logic, although eliminating injustice is far from being a core concern. Everything continues to revolve around figures: How many trees need to be planted? How many hectares need to be reforested? Technical strategies are obviously needed to combat soil erosion and deforestation. Paradoxically, however, farmers are for the most part not involved in developing these strategies. There is no sense of shared political responsibility to be discerned. The state has abandoned the farmers, and their fate is in the hands of NGOs and international organisations. The farmers are victims, who have to bear the responsibility; having become the target of development aid, they have to implement the technical solutions themselves. With no social, political, or economic justice in sight, injustice continues to prevail.

Abya Yala

Wallmapu and Ayiti, the Indigenous names of the territories cited as examples here, were marginalised—along with their inherent knowledge and practices—by the colonial mechanisms of modernity. The consequences of this are still visible today. Decolonial thinking starts by establishing this double fracture of modernity, drawing on the experiences, struggles, and knowledge of Indigenous and Afrodiasporic people in order to counter coloniality. Abya Yala, or the "living land", as the Kuna called America, accordingly becomes a place of pluriversality in which many worlds are possible—without inequality and exploitation.

Chris Pappan

FREE TO ALL, 2013, acrylic and gold leaf on wood, Chicago, 2013.

North American Native Museum NONAM, Zurich.

FREE TO ALL

For this artwork Chris Pappan, who considers himself Native-American, uses a historical photograph that depicts the North American state of Kansas as uninhabited territory. In so doing, he confronts the viewer with the myth of the "Wild West" and the reality of the destruction of Native American culture.

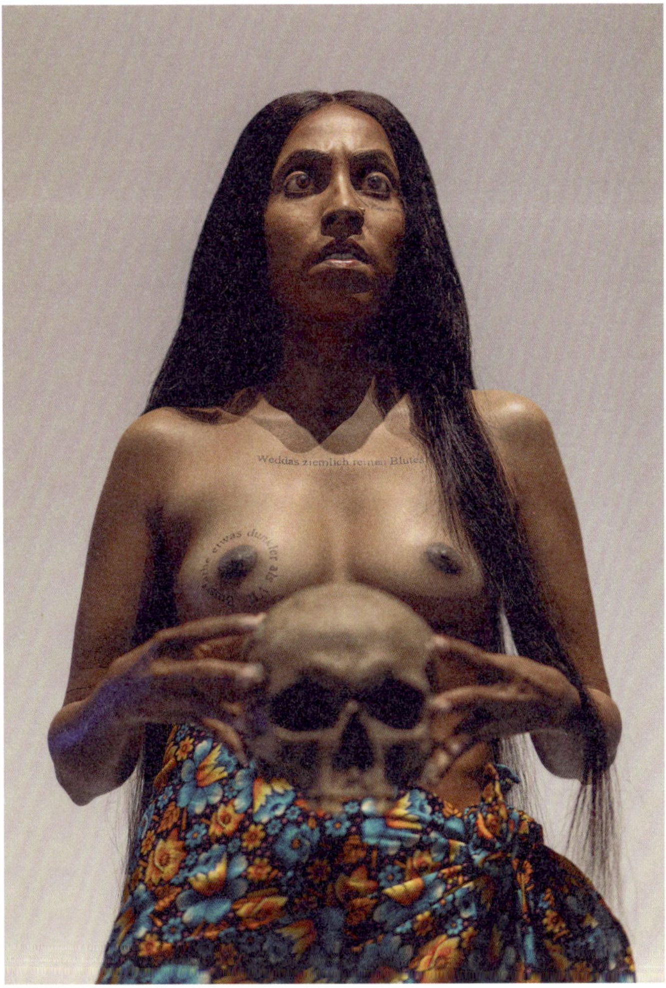

Deneth Piumakshi Veda Arachchige

Self-portrait as reparation—from a feminist point of view, from the exhibition *Voices from an archived silence*, a multimedia project curated by Vera Ryser & Sally Schonfledt, sculpture, 3D SLA print, 2020.

Photo: Silke Briel.

Dignity for the ancestors

For the exhibition *Voices From An Archived Silence*, Deneth Piumakshi Veda Arachchige created a sculpture with the title *Self-Portrait as Restitution—from a Feminist Point of View* (2020). It is based on her own body, which she deliberately exposes, as was common in many anthropometric photographs. In her hands, she holds a replica of the skull of an Adivasi man who was brought to Switzerland by the Sarasins. With this gesture, she wants to restore the dignity of her uprooted ancestors.

Cian Dayrit

Et hoc quod nos nescimus, 2018, embroidery on fabric (in cooperation with Henry Caceres).

Courtesy the artist and NOME Berlin, photo: Gianmarco Bresadola.

Counter-cartography

Philippine artist Cian Dayrit engages critically with geographical maps, the power relationships they reflect, and the relationships between (post)colonial exploitation, imperialism, and neoliberalism.

Heidi Amrein

studied archaeology and art history at the University of Lausanne and completed her doctorate on the subject of Roman glassware. She has taken part in numerous excavations in Switzerland and abroad, worked in Rome for several years, and taught various courses at the universities of Zurich, Bern, and Basel. As a curator at the Swiss National Museum, she has led various research, exhibition, and publication projects focusing on Roman and early medieval archaeology, cultural history, and the history of science. She has been the museum's chief curator and a member of the Management Board since 2010; her research interests include the history of the institution.

Marina Amstad

is a historian and exhibition curator at the Swiss National Museum. She studied history and Slavonic studies in Basel, specialising in modern and contemporary history as well as Russian linguistics and literature. She has worked on various exhibitions at the National Museum Zurich since 2016. She is co-curator of the exhibition *colonial—Switzerland's Global Entanglements*.

Tomás Bartoletti

is a global historian who has been working as a senior assistant and SNSF Ambizione research group leader at ETH Zurich since 2023. His research interests include the history of science and empire, the history of capitalism, and environmental history. His current research focuses on the history of pest control and commodity frontiers in the Global South, c. 1880–1930, and the history of Swiss science in nineteenth-century Latin America. In both these projects, Bartoletti explores the methodological intersections of material culture and transdisciplinary research, while also comprehensively integrating Indigenous perspectives.

Claudia Buess

is a historian and literary scholar who works as head of educational events at Mission 21, a faith-based development cooperation organisation based in Basel. She designs and hosts courses, webinars and conferences on topics, such as global justice, the historical entanglement of colonialism and mission, peace, (anti-)racism, transcultural exchange, and development cooperation. International exchange and the involvement of experts from Africa, Asia, and Latin America are central to her work. Buess is a trained mediator, who worked for many years as a Swiss diplomat in Bosnia-Herzegovina and Lebanon.

Jose Cáceres Mardones

is a historian and curator with a doctorate in history from the University of Zurich. He uses his academic and curatorial projects to explore options for decolonial practices situated between history and nature. The Decolonize Zurich collective, which he co-founded, is dedicated to the decolonisation of public space. In 2023 he took up a role as research assistant at PHZH, the Zurich University of Teacher Education.

Jovita dos Santos Pinto

is a PhD student at the Interdisciplinary Centre for Gender Studies (ICFG), University of Bern. Her research focuses on feminism, postcolonialism, Black Studies, and intersectionality. She is doing her dissertation on the history of Swiss public life from the perspective of Black women, based on theories of Black feminism. Her publications are on the themes of a postcolonial intersectional history of Switzerland and race as a historical category in Swiss history. She is also the founder of the platform histnoire.ch, documenting Black women who have featured in the Swiss public sphere.

Philipp Krauer

has been a research archivist at the State Archives of the Canton of Schwyz since 2021. He completed his doctorate at ETH Zurich in 2021 with a thesis on Swiss mercenaries in the Dutch colonial army. His research interests include global and colonial history as well as the history of knowledge and modern military history. He holds a master's degree in the history and philosophy of knowledge from ETH Zurich and a bachelor's degree in general history and German linguistics and literature from the University of Zurich. He was also one of the initiators of the public history project zh-kolonial.ch.

Georg Kreis

is a historian. Until 2011 he was a full professor at the University of Basel and head of the interdisciplinary Institute for European Global Studies, as well as chairman of the Federal Commission against Racism from 1995 to 2011. Between 2000 and 2004, he was head of the National Research Programme NRP 42+ on "Relations between Switzerland and South Africa", writing its final report in 2005. Kreis was editor and co-author of the 2014 handbook documenting Swiss history, which contains no references to colonial history. In 2023, however, he published the research report *Blicke auf die koloniale Schweiz*, which presents an overview of colonial Switzerland.

Monique Ligtenberg

is a historian who curated an exhibition on science and colonialism for the extract exhibition venue at ETH Zurich. She completed her doctorate at ETH Zurich in 2023 with a thesis on German-speaking doctors in colonial South-East Asia. She is also a founding member of the city tour project Zürich Kolonial.

Hannan Salamat

is a cultural scientist who has been working at the ZIID foundation since 2019. ZIID is a centre for inter-religious dialogue that promotes constructive and socially oriented discourse between religions and ideologies in Switzerland. Salamat is involved in various national and international projects promoting the pluralisation of art, culture, and the culture of remembrance; she is also a member of the Coalition for Pluralistic Public Discourse, a network that is active throughout Europe with respect to cultures of remembrance.

Bernhard C. Schär

has been SNSF Eccellenza Professor of History at the University of Lausanne since 2021. He leads an international research group that will be working on a collaborative history of Switzerland in Asia, Africa, Latin America, and Europe until 2026. Between 2020 and 2024 he advised the Swiss National Museum on the exhibition *colonial—Switzerland's Global Entanglements* (2024). During the same period, Schär was a member of the transdisciplinary project group Ein Wandbild kommt weg!, which uses artistic and scientific approaches to support the city of Bern in finding a democratic way of dealing with its colonial heritage.

Raphael Schwere

studied social anthropology and sociology in Zurich and conducted research as a predoctoral fellow at Frantz Fanon University in Hargeysa and at the Max Planck Institute for the History of Science in Berlin. He has co-curated exhibitions at the University of Zurich's Ethnographic Museum, the Uganda Museum in Kampala, and the Igongo Cultural Centre in Mbarara. His special areas of interest include practical knowledge, material culture, human–animal relations, and issues relating to cooperation between African and European museums. He is co-curator of the exhibition *colonial—Switzerland's Global Entanglements*.

Esther Tisa Francini

is a historian and head of the archives and provenance research at the Museum Rietberg in Zurich. At the Rietberg, she researches and communicates the history of the museum and the art market, the collections, and exhibitions of non-Western art. She pursues approaches to cooperative provenance research, object biographies and critical history of institutions, perspectives, and historiographies. She has also curated various exhibitions on the subject of provenance and the history of collections and museums. With Michaela Oberhofer, she's head of the Benin Initiative Switzerland (2021-2024).

Denise Tonella

studied history and cultural studies at the University of Basel and trained in film direction and production in Zurich and Munich. After producing several videos up to and including 2013, she worked as a curator and project manager for numerous exhibitions at the Swiss National Museum between 2014 and 2021, focusing on themes such as the Renaissance period, the history of the Middle Ages, and the women's movement. Tonella regularly teaches at universities and contributes her expertise to numerous specialist committees. She has been director of the Swiss National Museum since April 2021.

Marilyn Umurungi

is a curator as well as an artist and cultural practitioner. In her cultural and artistic educational work, she deals with mechanisms of inclusion and exclusion in European and Swiss cultural history—often set against the backdrop of topical social movements or popular culture. She is co-curator of the exhibition *colonial—Switzerland's Global Entanglements*.

Andreas Zangger

is a freelance historian based in Amsterdam. In 2010 he completed his doctorate on Switzerland's colonial links with South-East Asia. Since then, he has conducted in-depth research for various publications and exhibitions on Switzerland's international relations during the colonial era. He is currently writing a study of the eastern Swiss textile industry's global ties.

Swiss colony

The British colonial authorities granted Christoph von Graffenried (1661–1743) urban, market, and mining rights for the mineral deposits that were believed to exist in the region. Together with around 450 expats, he established the colony of New Bern at the confluence of the rivers Neuse and Trent in North Carolina.

Map of the *Schwytzerische Coloney*, Christoph von Graffenried, 1710, Burgerbibliothek of Bern, Mss.Mül.466 (3a).

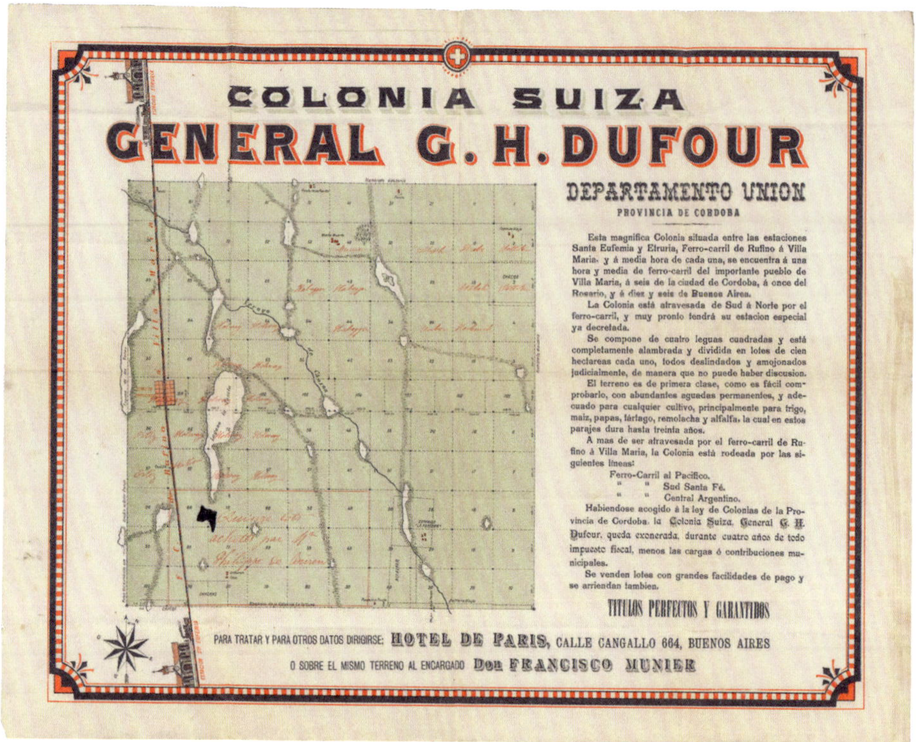

Advertisement for the Swiss colony "General Dufour"

When the countries of South America gradually liberated themselves from the Spanish and Portuguese colonial powers after 1809, free states governed by a *white* and Creole elite were established. With the help of European settlers, they sought to become "White" societies modelled on those of Europe.

Colonia Suiza, General G. H. Dufour, poster, Argentina, 1854–1888, Swiss Economic Archives, CH SWA HS 238 A 1.

Settler colony

Over twenty Swiss settler colonies were founded in Argentina between 1856 and 1896. Many of the settlers had emigrated to South America to escape poverty. However, they often failed to become rich in their new homeland, and it was only their descendants in the second or third generation that became more prosperous.

San Carlos colony, 1883, Swiss Economic Archives, SWA HS 238 A 3, no. 4.

Lenders

Fondation d'Haussonville pour le rayonnement del'Esprit de Coppet/Château de Coppet (Vaud-Suisse)

Collectie Wereldmuseum, Amsterdam

Koninklijk Tehuis voor Oud-Militairen en Museum Bronbeek, Arnhem

Mission 21, Basel

Herbarien Basel, Universität Basel

Historisches Museum Basel

Museum der Kulturen Basel

Schweizerisches Wirtschaftsarchiv, Basel

Öffentliche Bibliothek der Universität Basel

NOME, Berlin

Bernisches Historisches Museum, Bern

Burgerbibliothek Bern

Institut für Medizingeschichte, Bern

Naturhistorisches Museum Bern, eine Institution der Burgergemeinde

Schweizerische National-bibliothek, Graphische Sammlung, Plakatsammlung, Bern

Schweizerisches Bundesarchiv, Bern

Rätisches Museum Chur

Musée militaire et des toiles peintes de Colombier

Dr Patrick Minder, Fribourg

Bibliothèque de Genève

Musée d'ethnographie de Genève (MEG)

Finnish National Gallery, Museum of Contemporary Art Kiasma, Helsinki

Zentral- und Hochschulbibliothek Luzern

Musée d'art et d'histoire de Neuchâtel (MAHN)

Musée d'ethnographie de Neuchâtel (MEN)

Marie Irène and Bernard Mivelaz, Prilly

Yeo Workshop, Singapur

National Military Museum, Soest

Kanton Nidwalden, Staatsarchiv, Stans

Museum des Landes Glarus, Näfels

Musée historique de Vevey

Entomologische Sammlung der ETH Zürich

Erdwissenschaftliche Sammlung der ETH Zürich

Nordamerika Native Museum NONAM, Zürich

Schweizer Finanzmuseum, Zürich

Schweizerisches Sozialarchiv, Zürich

Tomás Joaquin Bartoletti, Zürich

Völkerkundemuseum Universität Zürich

Zentralbibliothek Zürich

Zürcher Hochschule der Künste, Museum für Gestaltung Zürich, Plakatsammlung

Artists

Cian Dayrit, Philippines

Chris Pappan, USA

Denise Bertschi, Switzerland

Deneth Piumakshi Veda Arachchige, France

Mathias Pfund, Switzerland

Dom Smaz, Switzerland

Maryanto, Indonesia

Sandeep TK, India

Sasha Huber, Finland

This publication is published on the occasion of the exhibition *colonial—Switzerland's Global Entanglements* at the Landesmuseum—Swiss National Museum Zurich, 13th of September 2024 to 19th of January 2025

Overall management	Denise Tonella
Exhibition curators and concept	Marina Amstad Pascale Meyer Raphael Schwere Marilyn Umurungi
Project management	Marina Amstad
Curatorial support	Heidi Amrein
Scenography	Alex Harb
Exhibition graphics	Selina Locher
Project coordination	Sophie Dänzer
Special advisor	Bernhard C. Schär, Lausanne University
Scientific advisory board	Carine Ayélé Durand Jose Cáceres Mardones Noémie Étienne Kwamou E. Feukeu Rohit Jain Georg Kreis Cassandra Mark-Thiesen Patricia Purtschert Anna Schmid Esther Tisa Francini Saoha Zala Roberto Zaugg
Project controlling	Sabrina Médioni
Cultural Services and museum education	Ashkira Darman Lisa Engi Vera Humbel
Technical organisation	Mike Zaugg Ladina Fait
Video installation	Lomotion AG, Detlef Vögeli
Films	Edgar Keller and Yoseph Agato Sareng Khalifa Hussein
Audio guide	kellerthurgau

Editor	Swiss National Museum
Coordination	Marilyn Umurungi
Concept and editing	Marina Amstad Raphael Schwere Pascale Meyer Marilyn Umurungi
Essays All texts have been translated from German, except for Tomás Bartoletti's, which was originally written in English.	Heidi Amrein Marina Amstad Tomás Bartoletti Claudia Buess Jose Cáceres Mardones Jovita dos Santos Pinto Philipp Krauer Georg Kreis Monique Ligtenberg & Bernhard C. Schär Hannan Salamat Raphael Schwere Esther Tisa Francini Marilyn Umurungi Andreas Zangger
Project coordinator, Scheidegger & Spiess	Anthonie de Groot
Translation, copy editing and proofreading	Tradukas GbR
Design	Bonbon, Zurich
Typesetting	Patrina Strähl
Lithography, printing and binding	Gugler GmbH, Melk, Austria

Verlag Scheidegger & Spiess
Niederdorfstrasse 54
8001 Zurich
Switzerland
www.scheidegger-spiess.ch

Verlag Scheidegger & Spiess received structural funding from the Federal Office of Culture for the period 2021–2024.

Museumsauflage
ISBN 978-3-905875-66-9

Verlagsauflage
ISBN 978-3-03942-211-1

With the kind support of

ERNST GÖHNER STIFTUNG

Stiftung Willy G.S. Hirzel